GOD'S GOLD MINES

C. Roy Angell

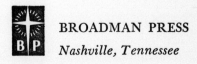

BROADMAN PRESS
Nashville, Tennessee

© 1962 · BROADMAN PRESS
Nashville, Tennessee

All rights reserved
International copyright secured

422–07221

Library of Congress catalog card number: 62-9194

Printed in the United States of America
10.N61K.S.P.

Contents

1
God's Gold Mines

In one of our daily papers there was a news item with this caption over it, "Is there a gold mine in your attic?" The story beneath was very fascinating. It read about like this. An elderly woman was poking around in her attic in search of something she needed. In an old bureau drawer she found a faded, yellowed envelope containing some valuable-looking documents. She looked at them for awhile and then decided she would take them to the bank to see if they were worth anything. She showed them to a teller and told him where she found them. It took him only a moment to say, "They may be *very* valuable; please wait just a minute."

He took them to an executive of the bank, who immediately came back with him to the window and invited the lady to come into his private office. You can imagine her astonishment when he told her they were bonds worth approximately $60,000 on the current market. He offered to sell them for her immediately if she needed the money. The writer of the article ended the story with this: "There may not be a gold mine in the attic of your home, but as Russell Conwell once said, 'There are acres of diamonds all around you that have not been discovered. Some of them may be in your mind and personality.'"

I think this story is able to set in motion our imaginations. I immediately thought of four places where there are undiscovered gold mines.

1

The first place is beautifully expressed by the psalmist, *"The earth is full of thy riches"* (Psalm 104:24). There is a television serial called "Wagon Train" that I often watch because my father was born in one of those covered wagons in the last century. Twenty miles was about all the distance those wagons could cover in a day. The hardships were innumerable, and danger was ever present. They crawled across our continent like snails. Today we know that, in the very mountains they struggled over so laboriously, there was hidden everything they needed to cross America in just a few hours.

Not long ago I stepped into a jet, and we raced the sun to San Francisco. It beat us only a few hours. I looked down on Death Valley as the stewardess pointed out to us a beautiful, clear, cold-water lake in the mountains on the very rim of Death Valley. If it had been discovered by our pioneer fathers, it would have saved the lives of literally thousands of people. We do not need to be reminded in this twentieth century that God has put a thousand gold mines in the material world, mines that we, with our half-open minds, have not found.

A scientist, in a magazine article, said that there would be enough power in a small lump of coal, if it were treated with radiation, to run all the railroads in the British Empire for a month. He added that there is enough power in one ounce of coal treated with radiation to run the largest steamship in the world across the Atlantic Ocean.

Another wrote that Monroe, Louisiana, is considered the capital of the Boeuf Basin. It was known for years as the Cotton Bowl of the South; then someone drilled for oil 2,500 feet down. His rigging was blown into little pieces, not by oil, but by gas. The gas was set on fire to keep it from injuring the cotton and endangering the lives of people. It burned for years before someone realized that it was a gold mine. Pipe lines were strung across the country—East, West, North, and South; and now thousands of people in the city of Miami cook breakfast with gas from the Boeuf Basin. This is just one paltry illustration of the undiscovered wealth that God has hidden beneath the surface of the world.

The second undiscovered mine is, in the words of Dr. Louis Banks, the *gold mine of humanity*. All of us have seen some boy or girl grow up without our even thinking that they might eventually become a great factor in the welfare of the world. For instance, I saw the picture of a sixteen-year-old boy some time ago in a magazine. The face was good and clean and strong. My attention was caught by the question above it: "Can you put a name under this picture?" It challenged me to study the picture for a little while, but I gave up and read the writing below the picture. It was the face of Joseph Stalin. I thought of the people who must have known him in his boyhood, maybe cuffed him around and mistreated him, never dreaming that the day would come when the brain hidden behind that innocent face would affect the lives of millions of people.

While I was pastor at Baton Rouge, a tow-headed, and most unpromising-looking, boy came into my study. He was a freshman at L.S.U. Embarrassed, he stammered out this question, "Doctor, do you think I could ever be a medical missionary?" I was sorely tempted to discourage him, but I thank my Lord that he didn't let me say the words out loud. The day came when I was sitting with the Baptist Foreign Mission Board in a meeting at Richmond to examine the candidates for appointment. I involuntarily stood up when this same erstwhile, tow-headed boy and his wife, a lovely girl, were presented by Dr. Maddry, Secretary of the Board, as applicants for the foreign field. He had graduated from one of the best medical schools. His face, which had changed, was good to look at. Intelligence and strength of character were written all over it. It made me realize afresh that we do not have eyes to see the gold mines that God has hidden in the minds and the lives of those around us.

The third gold mine is the *gold mine of prayer*. In the words of Jesus, we are told, "If ye shall ask anything in my name, I will do it." You would expect me, as a preacher, to say that prayer is the most powerful thing in the world. You would expect me to say that it can change anything; that it can release the imprisoned splendor of a human life; that it can break the power of cancelled sin; that it can furnish all the strength we need to conquer a bad habit and wipe out from our lives any evil intents; and that it can help us to overcome our biggest obstacles. I repeat, you would expect me to say that, but would you expect one of the world's greatest entertainers to say it? And would you expect one of Miami's most successful businessmen to say it?

Well, Eddie Cantor wrote it down about like this: "When I followed our armed forces, in the Second World War, around the world, I was advertised as a single act. But they had it all wrong. I never went out on the stage alone. Every night I prayed to my Heavenly Father to help me make those boys laugh and help me to break the tension that was tying them in knots. They were facing death every day. I never could have done my bit to help them without my silent partner." The man who recorded this story added that few people knew that Eddie Cantor had given away more than four million dollars to charitable organizations, especially to those which were working with children.

I sat in the plush office of a big businessman, who is a dedicated Christian, and heard him say, "Roy, the greatest thing in the world is prayer. God answers prayer. He answered mine when my boy was reported missing at the battlefront and presumed to be dead or captured. He brought him home. No one would ever convince me that it was not a direct answer to my earnest prayers." As I write this, there is a letter on my desk that restates his belief in the power of prayer. Here is a gold mine that so many people have never discovered. The Bible tells us plainly that often we do not have what we want or need because we do not ask.

The fourth hidden mine is the *gold mine of influence*. Most of us are too careless, or maybe just too thoughtless, about our influence. Some one said years ago, "Every man is some boy's ideal." That is at least partially true, but this is entirely true: oftentimes our unconscious influence is a tremendous factor in the important decisions that others make. Many of us learned in our school days the poem by Henry Wadsworth Longfellow:

> I shot an arrow into the air,
> It fell to earth, I knew not where;
> For, so swiftly it flew, the sight
> Could not follow it in its flight.
>
> I breathed a song into the air,
> It fell to earth, I knew not where;
> For who has sight so keen and strong,
> That it can follow the flight of song?
>
> Long, long afterward, in an oak
> I found the arrow, still unbroke;
> And the song, from beginning to end,
> I found again in the heart of a friend.

The little things that often seem so trivial to us may be important and big to someone else. Our attitude toward our church may be the deciding factor in the salvation of some-

one that knows us. The power of a church is largely made up
of the collective influence of its members. The greatest good
that a church accomplishes is by no means a result of the
power of the preacher and his sermons. The responsibility
of making a church a vital influence in the community lies at
the door of its leadership and constituents. A poem by Ed-
gar A. Guest "The Layman" made this live for me.

Leave it to the ministers, and soon the church will die;
Leave it to the women folk, the young will pass it by;
For the church is all that lifts us from the coarse and selfish mob,
And the church that is to prosper needs the layman on the job.

.   .   .   .

When you see a church that's empty, though its doors are open
    wide,
It is not the church that's dying; it's the laymen who have died;
For it's not by song or sermon that the church's work is done;
It's the laymen of the country who for God must carry on.

The last mine is the *gold mine of the gospel.* There is a
marginal translation of the sixteenth verse of the first chapter
of Paul's letter to the Romans: "I am proud of the gospel of
Christ for it is the power." I sometimes wonder just how
deeply we believe. If we claimed this power, we would be
better witnesses and more enthusiastic personal soul-winners.
I believe our preaching would have more zeal and fire.

In a number of places I have found this story by Joseph
Underwood. The minister's condemnation of sin and crime
was so severe that a gang of bandits swore to kill him. But
tension is not rare in South Africa, and this African evangelist, still vibrant with the fire of his own conversion from
heathenism, continued to cry fearlessly for repentance. The
bandits waited night by night for an opportunity to plunge

a dagger into the minister's back. But because of their schem-
ing and waiting, night by night they heard the preaching of
the gospel. It was at the end of the second week that a young
man rushed to the pulpit just before the service began. "My
sins, my sins," he sobbed. "Can God save a sinner like me?"

The preacher took the young man into his office and led
him to Christ as Saviour. After a prayer, the young man
shook from his sleeve a long dagger. "This dagger was in-
tended for your back," he told the minister. "But now that
Christ has saved me, I don't need it any longer. You may
have it."

Few men could be calm in a time like that, but the
evangelist replied simply, "Don't give it to me. Go put it on
the table in the auditorium and tell the people what happened."

To the congregation the young man said, "Many of you
know me. I am the leader of . . . gang." A gasp of horror
burst from the lips of the people, for this gang was one of
the worst in the whole Johannesburg area. "My gang swore
to kill this evangelist," the young man continued, "but, to-
night, Jesus saved me. I won't need this dagger any more."

When he had finished, thirteen other young men walked
forward and placed their knives and daggers on the table.
"He was our leader," one explained. "He wants to follow
Christ, and we will too."

The power of the gospel is an undiscovered gold mine.

2
Let Down Your Nets

There is a picturesque story in the fifth chapter of Luke's Gospel. It gives the setting for one of the most interesting miracles that Jesus ever performed. As we all know, some of Jesus' miracles were wrought out of compassion. It hurt him deeply to see someone suffering. He could not pass a blind man or a leper. He even stopped a funeral in the street.

Most of these were miracles of compassion. However, there were some miracles, such as this one, which had a deep purpose, a teaching purpose. Jesus was recruiting his disciples. They needed a miracle right down where they lived. The healing of the sick or the curing of a leper would not do as well.

The story itself has some humor. The crowd was pushing Jesus backward into the Sea of Galilee. He saw Simon Peter's boat close by, stepped into it, and asked Peter to push out a little way from the shore. He used the boat for a pulpit. The people stood on the slope where probably everyone could see him as he sat and preached to them. I am sure Simon Peter thoroughly enjoyed holding the boat steady and being in the spotlight with so big a crowd. I imagine he swelled with pride a little and felt very important.

However, his complacency was to be shattered in a few minutes, for, when the sermon was finished, Jesus turned and gave him an amazing command, "Peter, row out into the deep water and let down your nets."

I wish I could have seen Peter's face as he sat astonished, almost unbelieving. I am sure there came rushing to his lips the words he never spoke, "That would be useless, Master; you can't catch fish in the Sea of Galilee in the daytime." I imagine he had much difficulty in controlling his impetuosity and demurring with a gentle rejoinder, "Master, we have toiled all night and caught nothing."

Simon Peter was in a bad spot. He did not know how to refuse the Great Teacher. Yet, if he went out and let down his net, all of those expert fishermen along the shore would stop mending their nets and stare in amazement. You can hear one of them voice the sentiment of the others, "Has Simon lost his mind?"

I am sure he was thinking, "This man has lived in Nazareth, faraway from the sea all of his life. He doesn't know anything about fishing or he would never have made this foolish request." Finally he decided there was nothing else he could do. Since he could not voice these thoughts to the Great Teacher, his answer is important, one we should never forget, "Nevertheless at thy word I will let down the net" (Luke 5:5).

Dr. Hastings in his *Speaker's Bible* fills eighteen pages with this story and thinks this particular sentence is one that should ever be treasured by Christians:

Pause a minute and think about it before I turn to the biggest message in this miracle. Every one of us has faced some difficult task assigned us by our Lord and at times we have found some alibi or excuse that was usable. I hope that by and by we have been able to repeat the words of Simon, "Nevertheless at thy word. . . ."

The poet F. Cornish was so impressed that he wrote four stanzas to make it live:

The livelong day I toiled in vain,
  My net no fishes fill:
How can I dare to try again?
  Yet at Thy word I will.

How often shall my brother sin?
  Must I forgive him still?
Hard hearts can never pardon win:
  Lord, at Thy word I will.

How can I strive in aught to shine,
  So scanty is my skill?
"Be perfect"—the command is Thine,
  Hearing Thy word, I will.

Harder than any work, methinks,
  To suffer and be still:
Though at the thought the spirit shrinks—
  Lord, by Thy grace I will!

There are many other sentences in this story from which we have heard sermons preached, such as "Launch Out into the Deep," "Depart from Me for I Am a Sinful Man," and, the closing sentence, "They Left All and Followed Him"— great topics all. However, to me the most challenging message is the one that boils up out of the Master's command, "Let Down Your Nets." Notice that Jesus used the plural "nets," but Simon let down only *one* net. I am afraid we sometimes think that one assignment is enough and that God asks too much of us. Now, the emphasis in this sentence could well be put on the word *your*.

Dr. S. D. Gordon in his book *Quiet Talks on Service* said Simon was thinking that if he had only known Jesus wanted to go fishing he would have borrowed the latest patented nets, or at least he would have gotten some better nets—some that had been cleaned of the grass and the weeds. But Jesus had said, "Let down *your* nets." God wants us to use that which he has given to us, and Peter learned his lesson that day. We find later in the record that Peter looked down at a lame man at the Gate Beautiful and said simply, "Silver and gold have I none; but *such as I have give I thee.*"

He was using his own nets again.

Dr. James Parrish, vice-president of Stetson University, and one of the great preachers of the South, made this message live for all his audience when he spoke at the Florida Baptist Convention in Pensacola.

"I came from the country," he said, "and had never had the privilege of hearing any great preachers. So, when I finally got down to Stetson and found that Roland Leavell was coming to the campus for a revival, I was all agog with excitement and anticipation. The first night of the revival I was on the front seat, smiling and happy. Dr. Leavell was at his best, and the sermon was a masterpiece. But long before it was over, the smile had left my face.

"After the service, I went back to my room. I was miserable. The thought kept ringing through my mind, 'God doesn't need *me*. I could never preach like that. Maybe I have made a mistake, and God hasn't even called me to the ministry.' It was a long, miserable night.

"The next evening, I sat about midway, and once more there was no joy in my heart. The sermon was wonderful, and I was convinced more than ever that God just couldn't use me.

"The third night I was on the back seat, downhearted, as I listened to another powerful message. When it was over, I went out and lay down on my face in the campus grass and wept. I was ready to give up and go home, and then God seemed to speak to me. He quoted his own words from the first Psalm, 'He . . . bringeth forth *his* fruit in *his* season.'

"I lay there for a long time and finally said, 'Well, Lord, if you can use me, you can have all of me. I will use my little one talent to preach in some small country church and do my best for thee.' "

I think Dr. Parrish is still humbly amazed at what God can do with our talents when we can say, "Nevertheless, at thy word I will let down my nets." How beautifully this illustrates the great truth that God wants us to use whatever gifts he has bestowed upon us. To each of us he says, "Let down *your* nets." Both the Old and New Testaments are filled with illustrations of this great truth. Look for a moment at two.

Shamgar was an Israelite who lived in the time when the Philistines had overrun his country. The enemy had refused to let them have a blacksmith or make any weapons. All of their swords and spears had been confiscated. The Philistines allowed them to till the soil and raise a crop, and then they swooped down and reaped it. One day, when Shamgar was plowing in a field, some of his countrymen came running over the top of the hill and fled past him. He asked one of them why they were running.

He answered, "The Philistines are coming."

Shamgar gritted his teeth and asked, "How many?"

When he answered, "About six hundred," anger flared up in Shamgar, and he said to himself, "That's just about the right number." He unhitched the oxen and took the ox goad, which was the only weapon he had, and walked up to the top of the hill to meet the six hundred Philistines. He killed them all; he killed them with an ox goad. He used what he had.

Gideon's army was stripped down to three hundred. The Scripture points out that they were chosen because they had lapped water with their hands instead of lying down on their faces to drink. Then God gave to Gideon a strange command, "Gideon, send those three hundred, each with a trumpet and a pitcher containing a candle, to surround the Midianites," who were spread out across the Valley of Jezreel like grasshoppers or like the sands of the seashore. At a signal, they blew their trumpets, broke their pitchers, and yelled, "The sword of the Lord, and of Gideon." And the record reads "They stood every man in his place round about the camp." They used what they had. They let down *their* nets, and there was another victory for the Lord.

Paul had in mind this same great thought when he wrote, "And he gave some, apostles; and some, prophets; and some, evangelists; and some, pastors and teachers" (Eph. 4:11). The kingdom of God has a variety of needs. Paul didn't exhaust the list. He was not trying to exhaust it. He could have added a hundred more things that God needs. God needs every talent and every gift he has bestowed upon us. They are, in a sense, our nets. Let me mention just three.

First, God needs some *golden nets*. To some people God gives the ability to be financially successful. Jesus said, "To whom much is given. . . ." Paul wisely points out that the wonderful message of salvation must be taken to the faraway places, and then he challenges us with the question, "How can they go except they be sent?" There are many, many places where a golden gift from someone, to whom God has given much, makes the difference between life and death, between heaven and hell, for someone else.

Dr. W. F. Powell, of Nashville, related this incident. He was going down to his office one Monday after making a call on a family that was in sore distress, when a well-to-do merchant called across the street to him. "Dr. Powell," he said, "you preached a great sermon on heaven yesterday. But you didn't tell us where heaven is."

Dr. Powell said, "I looked at him and his fine clothes and his beautiful store filled with all the good things to eat that anyone would want, and I thought of that family in need. I answered him rather sharply, 'Come over here and walk a couple of blocks with me, and I will show you where heaven is not but where it could be.' "

Dr. Powell pointed to a little yellow house on the side of a hill and said to him, "In that house are two children sick in bed and a mother, who is so sick she should be in bed. There isn't one thing to eat in that house. There isn't a piece of wood or a lump of coal. Walk up there and take a good look at their needs. Fill their pantry full of food; send them a load of coal and a load of wood. Get someone to go up there to take care of them and cook for them for a few days, and you will find out where heaven could be."

The next day he came into Dr. Powell's study, sat down, and looked at him silently for a couple of minutes. Then he said in a husky voice, "I'm mad at you. Why haven't you told me before where there was trouble like that? I did everything you suggested and then some, and I will look after them until their trouble is over. I just came from there. They are all smiles. They couldn't thank me enough. Now you don't have to tell me where heaven is; a little of it is in my heart." He had let down *his* net, and God had filled his heart with joy.

Second, maybe your net is an *intellectual net,* made of the fine strands of clear thinking and good judgment. God has a great need for men like this in his kingdom, for it's big business. God needs stewards who can think clearly and have visions. The kingdom needs men who can see the danger spots and can guide his church around the ominous storms. I have known many men like this, and I have often thanked God for them. Let me name just one.

In my first pastorate, a large country church in eastern

North Carolina, there was a deacon named Steve Stafford. At a Saturday conference of about two hundred men, I asked the church to go on record favoring national prohibition which was to be voted on soon by Congress. Imagine my consternation and surprise when a man jumped to his feet and made a motion that we go on record *not* in favor of prohibition. At least a dozen voices seconded the motion. I am sure I turned pretty pale. And I confess I was about to tell them to amend that motion and include in it my resignation, when Mr. Stafford stood up smiling, looked around over the crowd, and then in a voice entirely void of any emotion said, "Brother Pastor, I move the matter be tabled." I don't think I ever looked at Steve Stafford after that without a feeling of deep gratitude and an impulse to thank God for him. He had let down his net.

Finally, there are some people whose nets God needs that I find no way to describe. They are the people who are not born leaders, wealthy, or brilliant. But they are loyal and faithful and useful workers in the kingdom. I am thinking of the eleventh and twelfth verses in the seventeenth chapter of Exodus:

And it came to pass, when Moses held up his hand, that Israel prevailed: and when he let down his hand, Amalek prevailed. But Moses' hands were heavy; and they took a stone, and put it under him, and he sat thereon; and Aaron and Hur stayed up his hands, the one on the one side, and the other on the other side; and his hands were steady until the going down of the sun.

Aaron and Hur, as good as they were, had no effect on the battle. Yet that battle would not have been won without their help. Moses could not have held up his hands all day. So they put a stone for him to sit on, and they held up his hands until the sun went down and the battle was won. Maybe that is your kind of net. It is, indeed, a net that God cannot do without.

Let me close with this illustration. I worked in the C. & O. railroad shops at Clifton Forge, Virginia, when I was little more than a boy. We had stripped an engine down to the frame and boiler and were beginning to build it over again. I noticed a machinist ream out the bolt holes in the heavy steel frame. Then he measured the hole carefully with a pair of calipers and made a bolt on his lathe to fit snugly in that hole. Sometimes it took a half-dozen trips between the lathe and the engine to get it to fit with precision.

One day I asked a fine Christian mechanic why they took so much pains with those bolts. He took his hat off and pretended to scratch his head as he stood looking at the new bolts. He said, "There's nothing much more important in that engine than those bolts. They hold the big driving wheels in line and keep down all the vibration in the engine. By and by, when the drivers and all the balance of the machinery is in place, those bolts will be invisible, but the engine would be useless without them. It would soon shake to pieces and the wheels would even jump the track." With a grin he turned back to me and said, "I often liken myself to those bolts. In my church I can't preach, I can't sing, I don't have much to give, I don't have enough business ability to help much, but I can be there and help hold the church together. The Lord knows, and the preacher knows, they can count on me."

In the words of Dr. Foote, "Take a look at yourself," and let down *your* net.

3
Lost—Something Precious

"The Lost Diamond" was the title at the top of an article in one of our newspapers. In substance it went like this. A diamond cutter was working on a very expensive diamond. He had fastened it in a small vise on his velvet-covered workbench. The diamond seemed to slip a little, so he gave the vise another turn. When he did, the diamond shot out of the vise, hit the ceiling, and ricocheted out of sight.

Since he was the only one in the room, he immediately locked the door and started to search for the diamond. He didn't anticipate much difficulty in finding it, but after a half-hour he became fearful and troubled. He searched every nook and corner. He turned over every piece of furniture, but he found no diamond.

The diamond cutter left his office, locked it after him, and went to the owner to report the incident. They came back and together searched the shop again, but to no avail. The owner trusted him implicitly and never for a moment even suspected him of having stolen the diamond. But the rule of this diamond factory was that anyone losing a diamond must pay for it out of his salary. So the owner and the cutter agreed that $60.00 a month would be subtracted from his salary until the cost price of the diamond would be paid in full.

After six months had passed, $360 had been subtracted from his salary. Then one day the cutter's telephone was out of order, and so a repairman was called. When he unfastened

17

the little square box from the wall, an outcry of astonishment burst from his lips, "Look what I found!" There was the big diamond! It seemed impossible that it could have hit that one tiny hole in the box for the telephone wire.

After reading the story, I sat awhile thinking about some other precious things that seem impossible for us to lose, and yet we do lose them or we have lost them or we may lose them yet.

I thought of the time Mary and Joseph lost Jesus at Jerusalem. They had gone a whole day's journey before they realized they had lost him.

I thought of the time that I carelessly lost my compass in the Devil's Swamp of Louisiana and came near losing my life because of my carelessness.

I thought of the story that Jesus told of the lost sheep and the lost coin. Then it was just a step to another realm in which too many of us lose some very precious things. Look at four of them.

First, we lose our sense of thankfulness. It is so easy to accept the precious gifts that God gives us daily and then forget to thank him. We get in the habit of saying "thanks" at mealtime. We learn some simple little blessing and, parrot fashion and often thoughtlessly, mumble it before we eat. We get up in the morning and fretfully hurry in our preparations to get to work. And we never stop to say, "Dear God, I thank thee for last night's rest and the joy of having something to do today." Someone does us a favor, and we forget to thank him; or we say some word of appreciation half-heartedly.

Dr. Chevalier Jackson told a story all across the country that emphasizes the value of gratitude. As you may remember, Dr. Jackson made two of the greatest contributions to medical science ever made in a century. He perfected the esophagoscope and invented the bronchoscope. They repre-

sented years of toil, fatigue, and patience. He used the esophagoscope first in a mining town. In this town, small lye tab-
lets, which looked so much like candy, were sometimes eaten
by the half-starved children. In his lectures over the country,
he told of an incident that happened in that mining town
and he labeled it "My Largest Fee."

Two Christian people went to visit a miner's wife who was
dying of pneumonia. They found the husband on the floor in
a drunken stupor and a little girl, who had eaten a lye tablet,
also on the floor nearly dead because she had been unable to
swallow any water for nearly a week. They brought her to
Dr. Jackson's office. When he inserted the scope, he found the
esophagus almost closed with a small chunk of food acting as
a cork in the narrow opening. After removing it, the nurse
held a glass of water for her to sip. The little girl expected it
to choke her and come back; but, when it went down, her
face lighted up with an inexpressible delight. She took another sip, then gently pushed the glass aside, and reached for
Dr. Jackson's hand. To his embarrassment and chagrin, she
covered it with kisses and then eagerly drank some more water, a glass of milk, and fell sound asleep.

We do not always see the hand behind the bounties, but
we never cease to thrill when we read the story of Simon
Peter and his earnest statement, "Thou art the Christ, the
Son of the living God." *He* recognized the God behind the
world.

Second, we lose our sense of humor. The loss of Will
Rogers was a severe blow to the world. He was teaching us
to look for the funny things in life. I heard him at the University of Virginia and saw him whirl that famous lariat,
stepping in and out of it. And, all the time, he kept us in an
uproar of laughter. He interspersed his humorous sayings
with some that were very serious and thoughtful. One of them

that has done me good was this: "Woe unto the business or professional man who loses his sense of humor. In the place of it he will have ulcers or a nervous breakdown."

Then he related this, that beautifully illustrates his statement about looking for the funny things in life. He said, "I was fishing down by the culvert the other day, when I heard a noise in the leaves. I went over to investigate and, lo and behold, there were two snakes; one of them had swallowed the other one's tail, and the other one had swallowed his tail. And I said out loud, 'Now, what's going to happen if they both keep on swallowing long enough?' I went back to my fishing, and, after a while, I returned to look at the snakes." Then with his inimitable drawl he said, "Sure enough, they were both gone."

Judge Culbreath lost one leg in the war, but despite this handicap he has kept his keen sense of humor and also has become one of Miami's outstanding judges. Speaking to the Brotherhood of our church, he began like this:

In the northern part of Florida there is a town named Chattahoochee, which is on the edge of the Eastern standard time zone. A few miles west is Marianna, which is in the Central standard time zone. A Negro man came down to the bus station at Chattahoochee to buy a ticket to Marianna. He walked up to the ticket window and asked, "What time do the next bus leave for Marianna?"

The prompt reply was, "Twelve o'clock."

"What time do it git to Marianna?"

The ticket agent answered, "Twelve o'clock."

The darky pushed his cap back and, scratching his head, said, "Boss, would you mind draggin' that through ag'in? I musta' missed something. What time do the bus leave for Marianna?"

Restraining a smile, the agent said, "Twelve o'clock."

"And what time do it git to Marianna?"

Again the answer was "twelve o'clock." The darky shifted from one foot to the other and looked bewildered. The ticket agent asked him, "Do you want a ticket to Marianna?"

After a moment the darky said, "No, sir, I don't believe I do, but if you don't mind I'll hang around awhile. I wants to see that thing take off."

As Will Rogers said, we need to keep our sense of humor; for, when we lose it, we may lose something precious.

Next, we lose our sense of responsibility. Paul stated it deftly when he said, "I am debtor both to the Greeks, and to the Barbarians; both to the wise, and to the unwise. So, as much as in me is, I am ready to preach the gospel to you that are at Rome also" (Rom. 1:14–15) . He didn't mean he had borrowed money from the Greeks and Barbarians and then felt he was in debt to them. He meant that, since he knew the power of the gospel of Jesus Christ, he owed them the chance to have the good news. In other words, he felt keenly his responsibility to everyone who was not a Christian. He must have been thinking of the words that Jesus spoke in the parable, "Go ye therefore into the highways, and as many as ye shall find, bid to the marriage" (Matt. 22:9) .

Recently I took some twenty of the weekly church bulletins that came to my desk and counted the number of people who had made professions of faith on a given Sunday. I was startled to find there were only nine. In one of those bulletins, the pastor had written this sentence: "In the last six months we have had only seven professions of faith in this church and I am deeply concerned. Please make this a matter of earnest prayer."

I thought of an Episcopal minister who had resigned. The vestry came together quickly and asked him, "What in the world do you mean? You're the best loved minister we ever had. The church is flourishing and it's fine. What in the world is the matter? Tell us, what's the matter?"

He said to them, "I've lost my prayer book."

They said in consternation, "Lost your prayer book? Why, we've got five hundred in the church. We'll buy you five hundred for yourself."

Then the chairman said, "There is something behind that sentence, Pastor—what is it?"

He said, "I've lost my prayer book. When I first came, you met with me in the vestry room before every service— great crowds of you. I walked into the pulpit, and you walked along with me. The whole church knew that we'd been praying together. A hush fell over it. It was easy to preach. But there hasn't been anyone at all lately. One by one, I've lost the pages out of my prayer book. Now, I don't have any at all."

Billy Graham, in his Miami crusade in March, 1961, sent cold chills up our spines as he said, "I came back recently from Africa, and I have bad news for you. We Baptist people think that we are doing a wonderful work in Africa and that we are winning the world for Jesus." Pounding the podium, he continued, "We are not winning the world. We are losing it! For every single convert we make for Christianity, Mohammedanism makes eight in Africa. We boast of having fourteen hundred missionaries scattered around the world. One single denomination has more than fourteen hundred in one little country in Africa."

Could it be possible that we are losing something very precious, our sense of responsibility to carry out the Great Commission?

Mr. Moody was holding a revival service in a large church. He asked the pastor to have all the Sunday school teachers meet him at supper on Wednesday evening. With all of his earnestness, he laid upon them the responsibility of reaching unsaved people. When he paused for a moment, one of the teachers stood up and smilingly said, "Mr. Moody, I am the happiest teacher in this Sunday school. Every person in my class is a Christian."

Mr. Moody thundered back, "You ought to be the *unhappiest* teacher in the world. You ought not to be able to sleep a single night until you and your class have brought to your classroom others who do not know Jesus Christ as Saviour." Every Sunday school teacher in the Southern Baptist Convention ought to hear and feel the challenge and take it to heart, "How can they be saved unless they hear?"

Finally, have we lost the sense of urgency? Mañana, "tomorrow," is a word that once was heard south of the border only, but the Rio Grande River was not wide enough to keep us from being infected. It's possible that we, with our "take-it-easy" philosophy, infected our neighbors south of the Rio Grande, instead of vice versa. We get so enthusiastic and impatient about minor things and put off until some more convenient season the precious things. Complacency is a vicious sin.

I received a wire recently that Deacon Wylie Johnson, of San Antonio, had just passed to his reward. My mind immediately went back to the day that I walked into his department store and told him of two young men who had just opened a new business down the street from him. I told him they were fine men but that neither of them was a Christian and that maybe a word from him would make it easier for me to lead them to Christ. A couple of days later, he called me back and, in dead earnest, said, "Roy, the afternoon you told me of those two young men, I went down to see them; but I'm not very good at talking to people about their souls. You do the talking, and I will pay the bills."

"What bills do you mean?" I asked.

He said, "Let's get about twenty men who are fine Christians and take them over to my ranch Saturday afternoon. I will get big, thick steaks and everything that goes with them. We will have a barbecue, and we will invite those two men to go along. Let's let them feel the fellowship and friendship of a crowd of Christians. In other words, I will set the whole stage, and you talk to them."

It is hardly necessary for me to finish the story, except to say that both of those men are deacons today in a Baptist church. Have we lost an important part of our heritage? Have we lost something that our forefathers had, something so very precious?

4
"Out of the Eater"

There is a good human interest story centered in the fourteenth chapter of Judges. It turns on the sentence, "Out of the eater came forth meat, and out of the strong came forth sweetness." I have read the story of Samson at least a hundred times without seeing the tremendous message for every one of us in this riddle that Samson gave the Philistines.

Of course, you remember the story. Samson fell in love with a Philistine woman and asked his father and mother to get her for him "for she pleaseth me well." His parents demurred and tried to point out to him the danger of such a marriage. They begged him to marry a woman of his own people, but he repeated obstinately, "She pleases me well." The whole thing smacks of this modern age of ours. However, it is lifted above the level of human life by the very next sentence that God wrote: "But his father and his mother knew not that it was of the Lord, that he sought occasion against the Philistines: for at that time the Philistines had dominion over Israel" (Judg. 14:4).

On one of the trips that Samson made down to see his fiancée, a young lion roared at him. The Hebrew reads "a young lion met him." Samson had no weapon, and so he fought the lion barehanded. Again God put a sentence there that we need to remember: "The Spirit of the Lord came mightily upon him." The writer wanted us to know this was part of God's plan and not just an incident in Samson's life.

Some weeks passed before Samson went by that spot again. In the meantime, the vultures and the beasts of prey had picked clean the bones of the lion and left the sun to bleach the carcass. Samson turned aside to look at the lion he had killed, and he was delighted to find that the bees had used the carcass for a hive. He took some of the honey and ate it as he walked along.

Following the custom of the time, preceding the wedding Samson had a party for the men. To give the party some spice and life, he made a bargain with the thirty young men who were his guests. He told them he had a riddle for them and, if they could solve it, he would give to each of them a change of raiment and a sheet. If they could not find the answer, they were to give him thirty changes of raiment and thirty sheets.

The riddle was "out of the eater came forth meat, and out of the strong came forth sweetness." The party was to last seven days, and the riddle was to have been solved in that length of time. They spent several days trying to find the answer but failed. On the seventh day, they threatened his bride-to-be that they would burn her and her home unless she found the answer. Scared half-to-death, she finally persuaded Samson to tell her the answer. Swaggering, the thirty guests came back to Samson and asked, "What is sweeter than honey? And what is stronger than a lion?" Samson was furious.

Again that sentence occurs, *"And the Spirit of the Lord came upon him,* and he went down to Ashkelon, and slew thirty men of them, and took their spoil, and gave change of garments unto them which expounded the riddle. And his anger was kindled, and he went up to his father's house. But Samson's wife was given to his companion, whom he had used as his friend" (Judg. 14:19–20).

But this revenge was not sufficient, and a little while later, at the time of the wheat harvest, he caught three hundred foxes. Then he turned them tail to tail and put a firebrand in the midst between each pair of tails. "And when he had set the brands on fire, he let them go into the standing corn of the Philistines, and burnt up both the shocks, and also the standing corn, with the vineyards and olives" (Judg. 14:4–5). Of course, this precipitated a war, in which Samson slew a thousand men and became a judge over Israel.

His riddle suggests this great message to me. *Out of the things that threaten our lives and happiness often come the sweetest blessings.* Look briefly at three of them.

The first is failure. Failure is a roaring lion. It is the eater that destroys many men. On the other hand, it often produces delightful sweetness. Some people destroy themselves because of failure; others find themselves.

"It is defeat," said Henry Ward Beecher, "that turns bone to flint, and gristle to muscle, and makes men invincible, and formed those heroic natures that are now in ascendency in the world—Do not then be afraid of defeat—You are never so near to victory as when defeated in a good cause."

"Failure is, in a sense," said Keats, "the highway to success, inasmuch as every discovery of what is false leads us to seek earnestly after what is true, and every fresh experience points out some form of error which we shall afterward carefully eschew."

"Be of good comfort, Master Ridley, and play the man," said Latimer, as he stood ready to be burned with his friend at the stake, "we shall this day light such a candle by God's grace in England as (I trust) shall never be put out." And every word had more influence than the preaching of a hundred sermons against the intolerance of the age. So incensed did the people become that, besides Cranmer, burned two years later, very few others were sacrificed. And of these it is said that they were secretly tried and burned at night, surrounded by soldiers, for fear of riots by the populace enraged at such injustice and cruelty.

Goldsmith was educated to become a physician but was a miserable failure. Three of his patients died. He sat for days in his office with no one wanting his services. He became dejected and despondent. To fill the hours, he wrote stories. Out of his failure as a physician came "The Vicar of Wakefield," "The Deserted Village," and a name that is immortal.

A. T. Stewart studied for the ministry but, because of his failure as a pulpit speaker, decided to teach. Here again he failed. Then he drifted by accident into a merchant's trade. He had lent money to a friend to open a store. The friend, with failure imminent, insisted that Stewart take over the shop as the only means of securing the money. He became a merchant prince, with branch stores in France, Ireland, and England. He saved literally thousands of lives by sending shiploads of food to the famine-stricken people of Ireland in 1846.

Stewart was appointed Secretary of the Treasury of the United States by President Grant. Congress, however, never ratified his appointment because he was engaged in importing goods from other countries and a law prohibited such appointments. He was of such stature that the President demanded Congress to repeal the law, but Congress refused. Yet out of the failure in preaching and teaching came one of the strongest businessmen and one of the sweetest spirits in the business world. "Out of the eater" came forth sweets.

Peter Marshall aspired to be a sailor, but the United States Navy refused to accept anyone under seventeen years of age. The British navy would accept men when they were sixteen. Peter Marshall was fifteen, but very tall for his age.

He falsified his age and was accepted in the British navy. They soon discovered the truth, and he was summarily dismissed. He went back home brokenhearted, sure that his whole life was ruined. In this hour of despondency, God laid his hand on Peter Marshall and led him into the ministry. He became world famous as Chaplain of the United States Senate. Across his life could be written the sentence: "out of the eater came forth sweets."

Further, disaster and hardship often open the door to the greatest blessings. Enterprise, Alabama, was known for a long time as the Peanut Capital of the world. It became the Peanut Capital after the boll weevil had eaten up all of the cotton in the county, and hard times had come knocking at the people's doors. Poverty, want, and suffering followed in the wake of the boll weevil. But there came a time when Enterprise erected a monument to the boll weevil because it brought about a variety of crops.

One of the finest and most successful businessmen in Miami said to me in a slow drawl, "The boll weevil ate up my college education, but I am not complaining, because I got an education the hard way and found my talents lay in the business world." Today he has amassed a million dollar fortune. He is thankful for the boll weevil and helped build the monument in Enterprise.

Another of Miami's big businessmen said to me, "When I was twenty-one, my father gave me a small farm. I didn't have enough money to buy cottonseed, so I borrowed it from my dad. I plowed the land and planted the seed. That fall I picked all of the cotton I had and sold it for fifty dollars. I left the farm and came to Miami." Today, he is a partner in one of the biggest business concerns in our city. He has been chairman of the board of deacons in our church and is loved by every one who knows him.

"Out of the eater came forth sweets" applies to both of
these men.

I heard of an amusing incident recently that illustrates
the same thought. A friend of mine went into the beautifully
appointed office of a successful manufacturer. In substance
my friend said, "While I waited for the owner to answer a
telephone call, my attention was attracted to a picture on his
desk. It was the photograph of a vicious-looking, ugly man. I
wondered why anyone would want such a face staring at
him continually. My curiosity went beyond bounds. When he
had finished his telephone call, I asked him if this was one of
his friends. His answer made me laugh. He exploded,
'Friend! Not on your life! That's the meanest man I ever
knew on earth, and I used to work for him. I keep his picture
here to remind me that if I don't make a success of this business, I have got to go back to work for that guy.' "

"Out of the eater came forth sweets." Out of the things
that appear to us to be the worst experiences and the most
terrible disasters and that bring to us the deepest heartaches
many times come life's greatest blessings.

Finally, look at suffering. Not always, but often, out of the
vicious eater come sweets. I say not always because, as a poet
expressed it, "sometimes we waste our pains." Let me refer to
Dr. Joseph Sizoo's message on "The Revolt Against Pain."
"In our clearer moments we know that suffering has a purpose; and that purpose is threefold. In the first place, some
suffering is punitive. As long as right is right and wrong is
wrong, men will suffer. There were three crosses on the hill
of Golgotha. Two men were nailed up there because of trans-
gressions." One of the thieves turned to his comrade and
spoke the truth for all time: "We justly." Take away punitive suffering and society cannot survive. We reap what we
sow, yet out of that unbearable suffering, out of that fearful

"eater," salvation came to one sinner. For Jesus said to him, "This day shalt thou be with me in paradise." "Out of the eater came forth sweets."

Again, some suffering is disciplinary. Paul said, "Whom the Lord loveth he chasteneth." Often we will open the door between us and God and listen to his still, small voice in the *hour of suffering only*.

In the fourth century Saint Augustine fell into mental anguish, but through that pain he became one of Christ's great saints. Saint Francis tossed on a bed of illness in the twelfth century crying out against his suffering, but through that anguish he turned to God and with thirteen young men helped to bring Italy to the feet of Jesus. In the nineteenth century Loyola fell wounded in battle and was tortured by terrible pain, but in that hour he drew from under his pillow a copy of the Life of Christ, was redeemed and walked out with five brave souls to bring Asia and Europe to the foot of the cross.

The man who asks to be released from suffering takes the winter coat out of seasons, the November winds out of the sky and rain-storms out of summer. Take away pain and you take the Bedford dungeon from the life of Bunyan, the scars from the face of Lincoln, the loneliness from the soul of Paul and the cross from the life of Jesus of Nazareth. There can be no great character without suffering.

"Out of the eater came forth sweets."

Third, some suffering comes to us because of human relationships. We make sacrifices and suffer for others. Crosses are often laid on our shoulders because of our love for others. It may be true that if there were no suffering there could be no love. As Abigail said to David, "We are bound in a bundle of life." We often suffer hardship for those we love. Savonarola, Dante, Paul, Lincoln, Jesus—all bore crosses that were laid upon them because of their love for others. Without the shedding of blood there is no remission of sins.

In Jesus of Nazareth you have the answer to the riddle of pain. The most revered image ever fashioned by human hands represents a living man, a village carpenter spiked to a cross of wood. After two thousand years, that living man, a village carpenter spiked to that cross of wood still lives and holds the adoration of untold multitudes. It is the most moving story ever written, every sentence of which pierces the human heart. Sixty generations ago that cross of wood was planted on a hill outside of Jerusalem, and today one-third of the population of the modern world kneels before it.

"Out of the eater"—namely, the Pharisees, the sinners of the world, Pontius Pilate, and the agony of Jesus in the garden of Gethsemane and Calvary—came God's great blessing to the world. Redemption and salvation followed the heartache of the disciples and the suffering of Jesus. To those who loved him, as his disciples and mother loved him, the torture of the cross was the worst possible disaster. Certainly, in part, it was brought about by vicious enemies, ugly jealousy, inexcusable meanness, and the sins of his time and ours.

That which seemed to be failure, disaster, and unjustifiable suffering—all are wrapped up in the death of Christ. Yet out of these horrible eaters have come the sweetest boon of life for all of us. The poet said it better than I can.

> I came to the Valley of Sorrow
>   And dreary it looked to my view,
> But Jesus was walking beside me,
>   And sweetly we journeyed through.
>
> And now I look back to that valley
>   As the fairest that ever I trod,
> For I learned there the love of my Father,
>   I leaned on the arms of my God.

. . . .

And if some day the Father should ask me
  Which was the best of the paths that I trod,
How quickly my heart shall make answer;
  "The Valley of Sorrow, O God!"

5
The Dark Mile

Dr. Richard Holt Hutton, one of the greatest preachers and writers of our time, told of a most interesting incident that he and a traveling companion had during a recent visit to Scotland. Sometimes they traveled on bicycles, sometimes on horseback, but most of the time they walked. In substance he said, "In one particularly interesting place there were many lakes, and beside one of them stood a picturesque little inn. We spent a delightful night, and in the morning we were ready to travel again. On our inquiry, the innkeeper said that the most beautiful lake in Scotland was Lake Lochy, about four miles away. He got a map and traced the path with his finger. It went around in a semicircle. I asked, 'Is that the only path?'

"He answered, 'There is another way, but no one goes there by choice. It runs through "The Dark Mile," which is a deep gorge.' I inquired why they called it The Dark Mile, and he answered, 'Well, it's just what the name implies. It's gloomy and dark and frightening; big overhanging ledges of rock are dripping water all the time. There is just a thread of a path through it, and the vegetation is pale and dwarfed. The whole thing is forbidding and foreboding. Stay out of The Dark Mile, for, I repeat, nobody travels it by choice.' "

Dr. Hutton continued, "I guess there is some of the boy in us after we are grown, for my companion nudged me and then asked the innkeeper to show us the path to The Dark

Mile. We found it about as he described it. In the very bottom of it my companion grabbed me by the arm, pointed straight up, and said, 'Look up; you can see the stars in broad daylight.' I remembered the old axiom 'when it is dark enough, you can see the stars.' We picked our way along through the gloom, and suddenly we came out of the gorge. And there, spread out before us and surrounded with mountains, was beautiful Lake Lochy. Both of us gasped at the never-to-be-forgotten sight. Then my companion spoke in subdued tones, 'I don't believe that we would ever have appreciated the beauty of Lake Lochy if we hadn't traveled The Dark Mile.'

"That night I wrote down in my diary three sentences: 'Nobody travels The Dark Mile by choice. When it's dark enough, you can see the stars. We never would have appreciated the beauty of Lake Lochy had we not traveled The Dark Mile.' "

I laid the story down and sat there thinking what a beautiful sermon that incident preaches, for the three statements sent my mind to a dozen passages of Scripture. Look at a few of them that illustrate these sentences.

First, nobody travels the dark mile by choice. Moses was pushed into his first dark mile when he killed the Egyptian and had to flee the court of Pharaoh. His second one came when God told him to go back to Egypt, face Pharaoh, and lead the children of Israel out of Egypt. I am sure the cold perspiration stood out all over him when he stammered and stuttered that he couldn't do it. He found himself in another dark mile when he and the Israelites came to the shores of the Red Sea and then saw the dust clouds rising in the rear as Pharaoh's chariots, horses, and crack soldiers bore down upon them.

I once heard a speaker relate a humorous modern version

of what happened at the Red Sea. A little boy came home from Sunday school, and his father asked him what the lesson was about that day. The boy told him it was about the children of Israel crossing the Red Sea. Then the father said, "Tell me how it happened."

The boy's eyes sparkled as he answered, "Well, the teacher said Moses and the children of Israel got in a trap. They came up to the Red Sea and there wasn't any bridge and Pharaoh's army was chasing them. So Moses took his walkie-talkie and called the engineers and told them to come quick and put a pontoon bridge across the Red Sea. When they had the pontoon bridge in place, then the children of Israel marched across without getting their feet wet. When they got on the other side, they began to sing and shout and celebrate. One of the Israelites touched Moses on the arm and pointed back to the pontoon bridge. Pharaoh's army was marching across it, but Moses grabbed his walkie-talkie and called for the demolition squad. They came on the double and blew that bridge into smithereens, and Pharaoh's army got drowned."

The father tried to keep his face straight as he asked, "Son, are you sure that's the way the teacher told that story?"

The boy looked down at his shoes and mumbled, "Well, not exactly. But, Daddy, you never would believe it the way she told it."

Maybe Moses' darkest mile came as he descended Mt. Sinai and heard the shouts of the people singing and laughing and dancing around a golden calf. Certainly it could be written across these experiences that "nobody travels the dark mile by choice."

Joseph had his dark miles, also. For example, he was falsely accused by the wife of his master in Egypt and thrown into prison for life.

The life of David, likewise, was full of dark miles. Maybe the darkest was the day his favorite son hung by his hair in a tree on the battlefield, his body filled with darts and arrows and spear thrusts. Surely, he wouldn't have traveled that dark mile by choice.

Paul's life was one long series of dark miles. We see him stumbling along that road to Damascus completely blind, because the light of heaven had struck him. Time and again he was strapped to the whipping post, and forty stripes, save one, were laid upon his back. He was shipwrecked, put in prison, and finally led out to kneel before the executioner's block.

From these grand old soldiers of our Heavenly Father, we can learn a lesson—namely, that few of us will ever walk through life without finding at least one dark mile. Most of us will find too many of them. There was one, and only one, who deliberately chose the dark mile. He could have called down a legion of angels. Instead, he said, "For the joy that is set before me I will climb the hill of Calvary."

When it is dark enough, you can see the stars. In the first verse of the sixth chapter of Isaiah, we find these words: "In the year that King Uzziah died I saw the Lord sitting upon a throne, high and lifted up; and his train filled the temple." Apparently, Uzziah was Isaiah's idol. His death spoiled Isaiah's plans for life. It was a dark mile for Isaiah; then, in some way, God revealed himself. How we wish the great old prophet had gone into more detail. He did, however, give us one picture that this world needs today. The vision he saw was a picture of God on a throne, high and lifted up. He saw all of the heavenly hosts bowing before God and offering obeisance. It was a picture of the *God of authority*.

Is it possible that we preachers overemphasize love as the greatest attribute of God and minimize too much the author-

ity of God? When it was dark enough, Isaiah saw God as he
really is—a God to be adored, obeyed, and loved. A few sentences later in the chapter, God asks, "Whom shall I send,
and who will go for us?"

Then Isaiah said, "Here am I; send me."

Jesus said to his disciples, "If you love me, you will keep
my commandments." Do we think of God in terms of loving
authority? Have the words of Jesus—"He that loves me will
keep my commandments"—sunk into our souls? Do we accept his authority with unquestioned obedience?

*Finally, "we never would have appreciated the beauty of
Lake Lochy had we not traveled The Dark Mile."*

A grand old preacher said one day, "If I could have been
with Jesus for just one hour while he was here on earth, I
would choose the hour after his resurrection when he appeared to the disciples, or rather to one disciple, Thomas.
You remember he appeared to the ten disciples when
Thomas was not present; and when they told Thomas, he
wouldn't believe it. 'But he said unto them, Except I shall
see in his hands the print of the nails, and put my finger into
the print of the nails, and thrust my hand into his side, I will
not believe. And after eight days again his disciples were
within, and Thomas with them: then came Jesus, the doors
being shut, and stood in the midst, and said, Peace be unto
you. Then saith he to Thomas, Reach hither thy finger, and
behold my hands; and reach hither thy hand, and thrust it
into my side: and be not faithless, but believing. And
Thomas answered and said unto him, My Lord and my God'
(John 20:25–28).

"I think Thomas saw Christ in all of his glory for the first
time. All of the disciples had just walked through the darkest
mile of their lives, and apparently for the first time they saw
Jesus as the Son of God and the Saviour of the world. It was

after this that the Master said to them, 'Go into all the world to every nation and tell them the story of God and his love.' "

Since there is no escape for most of us, no way around this dark mile, there are two things that we need to do.

First, we should put the dark mile into our life's budget. Jesus told one man who would follow him, "The foxes have holes, and the birds of the air have nests; but the Son of man hath nowhere to lay his head." To another he said, "For which of you, intending to build a tower, sitteth not down first, and counteth the cost?" We need to build our spiritual reserves in order that we may have strength and a sense of security when, suddenly, we are pushed into some heart-breaking pit of darkness.

Second, we need to make friends with him who said, "I am the light of the world." You remember that when Jesus went back to his home town of Nazareth, he stood up to read from the Scriptures, "And there was delivered unto him the book of the prophet Esaias. And when he had opened the book, he found the place where it was written, The Spirit of the Lord is upon me, because he hath anointed me to preach the gospel to the poor; he hath sent me to heal the broken-hearted, to preach deliverance to the captives, and recovering of sight to the blind, to set at liberty them that are bruised." And when he had finished reading, he said to them, "This day is this scripture fulfilled in your ears" (Luke 4:17–18, 21).

Plainly and beautifully Jesus stated that a part of his great mission was to walk through the dark miles with the people who would follow him. He did not say it here only, but again he confirmed the same promise to his disciples as they were about to carry out the Great Commission. His words are very precious to all of us, "Lo, I am with you always." The dark mile will not be nearly so dark and gloomy and forbidding if we have the sweet assurance that Jesus will walk all the way with us. "Yea, though I walk through the valley of the shadow of death, I will fear no evil: for thou art with me; thy rod and thy staff they comfort me."

6
Our Urgent Needs

I recently read two interesting and delightful messages on the subject of man's great needs. One was written by Dr. Hugh Miller, one of our finest contemporary authors. He listed four things which he considered to be our greatest needs: work, play, love, and faith.

The other was written by Dr. Robert J. McCracken, of Riverside Church, New York. His sermon was entitled "What Christ Undertakes to Do for Us." He presented four things that he felt we need so much, and that God alone can give us: (1) "Christ gives us a world we can live in." (2) "He gives us a self we can live with. Self-weariness, self-distaste, even self-hate are common." (3) "He gives us a cause we can live for." (4) "He gives us a Master to follow and serve."

After reading both of those wonderful chapters over the second time, I suddenly realized that all of the things these eminent authors had felt to be the most needful things for us were included in the Master's last talk with his disciples. In his touching discourse in the fourteenth chapter of the Gospel of John, Jesus was giving them their final instructions. Two or three times he tells them he is leaving them and going back to his heavenly home. He ends every reference to his departure with an assurance that they will be supplied with the things they most need. In substance he said, "I am leaving you a tremendous task—the establishment of the kingdom of God on earth. You are to be my servants and my witnesses, and there are some things that you will constantly need. I promise you that they will be supplied."

I have selected the four great needs on which I think Jesus put the most emphasis.

The first need is *work* and a cause to work for. Both of the authors whom I just quoted included this one. Jesus said, "He that believeth on me, the works that I do shall he do also; and greater works than these shall he do; because I go unto my Father" (John 14:12). In other words, he was giving them a cause to work for; a cause that would challenge them to do their very best; a work that would be a blessing to their fellow men and bring glory to their Heavenly Father. When God created us in his likeness, he put in our deepest souls the demand that our work bring to us the satisfaction of knowing that it was worthwhile.

John Wanamaker illustrated it splendidly. He said that his father owned and operated a big brickyard. One day he needed a man, and so he ran an ad in the paper to that effect. Four young men were waiting the next morning when he got to the office. He took them to the window and pointed to a large pile of bricks in one corner of the brickyard. He told them to take four wheelbarrows and move that pile of bricks to the next corner and stack them carefully. So they shucked off their coats, rolled up their sleeves, and went to work.

About the time they finished, he walked out to them and said, "Move them to the next corner and stack them carefully over there." They looked at him with a question in their eyes, but they proceeded to move the bricks. When they had finished, they came up to the office.

Once more he took them to the window and said, "Move them over to that other corner and stack them again." They

shifted from one foot to the other and decided again not to
ask any questions but to go and move the bricks. When they
had finished, they returned to the office, dripping with perspiration. Mr. Wanamaker said to them, "Move the bricks
back into the corner where they were at first."

Three of the men went back to the yard, but one of them
lingered. After a moment he said, "Mr. Wanamaker, I thank
you very much for giving me a day's work. I needed it and
I appreciate it. But life is just too short for me to work at
something that isn't of any benefit to anyone."

With a smile, Mr. Wanamaker walked over and put his
hands on the young man's shoulders. He said, "You are the
man I am looking for. That brick business was just a test.
You passed. Come in tomorrow morning and go to work, and
it won't be moving bricks."

Jesus was saying to his disciples, "My Father works and
I work and you must work. You will have the satisfaction of
knowing that you are going to do great things for God, even
greater things than I did because my time is limited, limited
to three short years. You will be challenged continually to do
the impossible. You will be hated, despised, and spat upon;
but you will also be the means of saving souls and saving
lives. Your joy will be full."

The second great need that Jesus mentioned was the need
of *communication* and the promise that the channel would
always be open between his disciples and their Heavenly Father. He stated it like this, "And whatsoever ye shall ask in
my name, that will I do, that the Father may be glorified in
the Son. If ye shall ask anything in my name, I will do it"
(John 14:13–14).

I listened recently to an address made by our ambassador
to England. Among other things, he said that one of the sacred privileges of an ambassador was that of uncensored

communications with his government. The mail pouch that came from the Pentagon or from the President of the United States would be sealed before it left our country, and that seal would not be broken until it reached him in England. All other mail from one country to another might be opened by the post office or the government authorities if there was something suspicious about it. But the pouch that carried his letters to *his* government, as well as the ones that came to him from his government, must never be touched or its contents perused. This, of course, is international law and is observed religiously by every civilized country.

John recorded the same thought when he wrote in the book of Revelation, "Behold, I have set before thee an open door, and no man can shut it." I think we should keep in mind, however, as we read Jesus' promise to his disciples— "Ask anything in my name and I will give it to you"—that he was talking *here* to his disciples only. I have never thought of this particular passage as pertaining to everyone. These were special ambassadors, and special privileges were given to them just as special privileges are given to our nation's ambassadors today.

Of course, in other places references are not always to special emissaries, and all of us agree that the privilege of prayer is one of our greatest needs. One of the sweetest promises of God's Word is that he will hear, and answer, our prayers. To be sure, sometimes he says, "No," but that open door which no man can shut belongs to all of us.

The privilege and power of prayer were recently brought home to me by a fine young pastor in South Carolina, whom I was helping in a revival. He said, "Brother Roy, I saw a miracle; *I actually saw a miracle.* My father was an alcoholic. He didn't stay drunk, but periodically he was overcome by a thirst for whiskey. Sometimes he fought it off for weeks but finally lost the fight. I was home for Christmas during the last year of my seminary work, and Dad said to me, 'Son, you are going to be a pastor soon, and you just can't have a drunken daddy, so I have quit. I will never get drunk again.'

"I went back to the seminary happy and hoping that he could keep that promise. He did keep it for several months, but on the day I came home, after graduating, I found him sitting by the dining room table with his head down on his arms. His face was covered with tears as he looked up at me and said, 'It happened again.'

"I sat down by him and talked with him for awhile, and then I asked him to please let me pray with him and for him. He had always told me before that he would do his own praying, so this time he startled me when he bowed his head and said, 'Son, please pray for me. Please pray for me every day.'

"That was the last drink my father ever took. That was nine years ago. He has become a Christian of the first magnitude. He has been elected a deacon and superintendent of a department in the Sunday school of his church." With a voice that was a little husky, this young minister continued, "Prayer changes things. God still works miracles. I can stand in my pulpit in the church and say with deep conviction, God answers prayer. He can change your life if you will pray to him."

Without any fear of contradiction, I say most emphatically, here is one of man's greatest needs—the need for communication between God and man.

The third great need is *love*. "Jesus answered and said unto him, If a man love me, he will keep my words: and my Father will love him, and we will come unto him, and make our abode with him" (John 14:23). Yes, we need to know that God loves us and that God wants us to love him. There is no way to tell the story of Jesus, not even half of the story, and leave out the word "love." It often has been called the very center of the gospel.

Certainly Paul considered it so. We need read but the first two verses in the thirteenth chapter of 1 Corinthians to realize how he evaluated love. "Though I speak with the tongues of men and of angels, and have not charity [love], I am become as sounding brass, or a tinkling cymbal. And though I have the gift of prophecy, and understand all mysteries, and all knowledge; and though I have all faith, so that I could remove mountains, and have not charity, I am nothing."

J. Winston Pearce tells a touching little story of a family and their morning devotions. The children, the mother, and the father took turns reading the Scriptures. One morning the four-year-old insisted that she be allowed to read the Bible that day. The other children ridiculed the idea and said the younger child could not read. The wise mother intervened, and the youngest was allowed to try her reading skill.

She opened the book to Genesis, underlined a verse, and then quoted a verse that she had learned in Sunday school, "God is love." She turned to Psalms, underlined another verse, and quoted the verse again, "God is love." She then turned to Matthew and quoted the verse again, "God is love."

This was more than the older brothers and sisters could stand, and they said, "You see, we told you she couldn't read the Bible." The mother very wisely replied, "Yes, she can, for when we really learn to read the Bible, it says 'God is love' on every page."

One of the presidents of the Southern Baptist Convention related this incident: "My boy and I were attending a large religious meeting in the auditorium in Houston, Texas. On the platform were a number of prominent men. Among them sat Dr. Truett, who was one of the speakers. I said to my twelve-year-old son, 'There are two good men sitting side by side up there. Dr. Truett is president of the Southern Baptist Convention, and the man by him is president of the Cattlemen's Association. The cattleman is immensely wealthy and one of the best men that ever lived. Which one of them would you rather be?'

"He looked at both of them keenly for a few moments and then said, 'I don't want to be president of either one of those things, but I would rather be Dr. Truett than anybody in the world.'

"Quietly I asked why.

"His answer was a classic: 'Because everybody in the world loves Dr. Truett, everybody that knows him loves him, and that must make life so happy for him.' "

Yes, we need to be loved. God created us with a great capacity in our hearts for love. We need paternal, we need maternal, we need fraternal—love. We need the kind of love that a boy has for the girl of his dreams, and the kind a girl has for the boy of her dreams. God made us that way.

The last great need of Christians is the *security that only our faith in God can give.* "Peace I leave with you, my peace I give unto you: not as the world giveth, give I unto you. Let not your heart be troubled, neither let it be afraid" (John 14:27). Let me quote from Dr. McCracken again, as he talks about this world and God's ownership and governorship of it:

I am not of a mind to quote, as though it were the last word on the subject,

> God's in his heaven—
> All's right with the world!

I am not forgetting that under the strain of the things that have happened in the world of our time—two global wars, the cruelty, the mass bombing; the things our enemies did to us, Buchenwald and Belsen; the things we did to them, Hiroshima and Nagasaki—there are people who find it hard to credit the testimony of Jesus that behind this scheme of things there is One who loves and cares, and who are tempted to conclude that the universe is a blind machine, started by nobody, attended by nobody, interested in nobody.

Gabriel Marcel, the French philosopher and dramatist, has a character in one of his plays say: "Don't you feel sometimes that we are living . . . in a broken world? Yes, broken like a broken watch. The mainspring has stopped working. Just to look at it, nothing has changed. Everything is in place. But put the watch to your ear, and you don't hear any ticking. You know what I'm talking about: the world, what we call the world of human creatures. . . ." It seems to me it must have had a heart at one time, but today you would say the heart has stopped beating.

Jesus was promising them the very thing that Paul wrote in Romans 8:28: "And we know that all things work together for good to them that love God, to them who are called according to his purpose."

A splendid illustration of the kind of security that Jesus was talking about happened in the Panic of 1893. Philip Armour, of Armour Packing Company, was at that time just building the great packing concern. He was a good Christian man in whom every employee had utmost confidence. Close by his little factory was a bank, in which Philip Armour was a director and in which his employees kept their savings.

The panic brought a run on the bank and forced it to close the doors at noon one day. They didn't have on hand sufficient cash for those who wanted to draw out their money. The frantic workers came running back to the plant, hysterical and in tears.

When Mr. Armour was told of the situation, he immediately came out on the high steps of his office and lifted his hands for silence. Then, with a smile on his face, he said, "Please don't be afraid. I make you this promise—I personally will see that not one of you will lose a single penny of your savings in the bank."

A murmur went up from the crowd. The murmur swelled into a roar, and the men threw their hats into the air. They rushed up the steps, took Mr. Armour on their shoulders, and carried him back into the big plant. And as they marched, they sang and shouted their love and appreciation for him.

It's a promise like this that was in Jesus' mind when he said, "Let not your heart be troubled: ye believe in God" (John 14:1).

7
Divine Roadblocks

Recently while traveling up U. S. Highway 1, I saw ahead of me a long, long string of cars that had stopped. I pulled my car up behind the last one and turned off the ignition switch. For nearly half an hour, we sat while the cars stacked up behind us as far as I could see. I guessed there must have been a wreck or a bridge out to cause a roadblock like this.

Finally, we moved ahead very slowly. Of course, we were all curious about what had caused the delay. I had traveled about half a mile when I came to a small group of people and one highway patrolman standing near the road. But there was no sign of a wreck, nor was there a bridge out. We were not allowed to stop or ask any questions, so we drove on and never knew what caused the roadblock. It just didn't make sense. And the thought came to me that there are a lot of things in life that just don't make sense.

Let me quote some paragraphs from Dr. Joseph Sizoo's sermon "When God Hides."

The person is not normal who is not sometimes staggered, whose soul is not sometimes chilled by events which tear at his being as a fox gnaws at a foot caught in the jaws of a steel trap. There are occasions when life does not make sense.

Here is that embittered soldier I met on Heartbreak Ridge in Korea with whom I had been talking about the events of life. He looked at me sharply and broke out with, "I'll tell you what's the matter with the world; your God has let us down."

There is that university student who had come to the end of his academic career. He had made a brilliant record, won every prize, earned and carried away every honor. The following week there was awaiting him a promising and lucrative position. The next morning he was to be married to his childhood sweetheart. Then on his way to commencement he was killed.

Here are two godly people whom I know very well. They fell in love, were married, and set up a Christian home. Then they prayed long, long hours for a little child, and at last, when the child was born, it was Mongoloid.

I am thinking of that man whom I visited often in the hospital. He had had thirteen operations and thirty-nine blood transfusions. One day he said to me, "I do not complain, but sometimes things do not make sense. I know all of this will end in death. I want it, but it won't come."

There is that British sea captain Sir John Hawkins who sailed his ship along the African coast kidnapping Negroes to sell to the slave trade. When he captured them, he chained them to the deck of his ship. And then he christened his ship "The Jesus," and God did nothing.

Dr. Sizoo's illustrations bring vividly to mind a classmate at Richmond College whose name was Johnny George. He was captain of the baseball team, captain of the football team, president of the class, and a member of the debating team. He was a brilliant student and was held in highest esteem by all of his classmates. A few months after he was graduated, he died of cancer. Dr. George McDaniel, preaching his funeral service, used the same sentence, "His untimely death does not make sense to you, his classmates, but remember, we cannot understand all of God's ways. Maybe he needed Johnny George in eternity."

In the Central Baptist Church fifteen years ago, we had a tenor soloist with a marvelous voice and a dedicated heart. I do not believe I ever heard anyone sing who stirred the souls of our congregation, as well as my own soul, as young Ernest

Allen. Everybody loved him and grieved when they remembered that he had leukemia.

I sat beside his hospital bed the day before he died and had no answer for his heartbreaking question, "Doctor, tell me why this has to happen to me. God gave me everything—a lovely wife, adorable twins, a church full of people that love me, and such wonderful prospects in business. Why do I have to die now? Please tell me why." I couldn't answer his question; but, as I left the hospital, I was saying to myself again, "It just doesn't make sense."

How many times have we seen something so wicked and so atrocious that we wonder why God allows such a thing to happen. I suppose that question is as old as the human family, for it is implied or stated in varying ways throughout the whole Bible. Look at these two instances in the Old Testament.

Gideon was threshing his wheat in a secluded nook in the mountains to hide it from the Midianites. Suddenly an angel stood by him and said, "The Lord is with thee, thou mighty man of valor. And Gideon said unto him, Oh my Lord, if the Lord be with us, why then is all this befallen us? and where be all his miracles which our fathers told us of, saying, Did not the Lord bring us up from Egypt? but now the Lord hath forsaken us, and delivered us into the hands of the Midianites" (Judg. 6:12–13).

Defiantly Gideon pointed through a little opening in the rocks and said, "Look at that plain of Esdraelon. There was a time when the dust from a hundred threshing floors went up to heaven as oxen and men tramped out the wheat and threw it with shovels into the air so that the wind could blow away the chaff. Today there isn't a single one down there, and I am hidden here in this little pocket in the mountains beating out my wheat by hand because the oxen have been stolen from us. How can you stand there and tell me God is with me?"

To Gideon it just didn't make sense.

Elijah stood on Mt. Carmel and teased the prophets of Baal. He told them to call louder on their gods to send fire and burn up their offerings. He laughed at them and said, "Your gods are asleep, or maybe they have gone hunting. Or maybe they are on a visit somewhere. Call again!" Then, late in the evening, he lifted his arms to heaven and asked God to send fire and accept his offering. God sent down fire that burned up the offering and the stones of the altar and licked up the water that ran into the trench.

Then in triumph Elijah said to his servant, "Go and look over the Mediterranean and see if there is a cloud."

After several trips, the servant came back to report, "There is a cloud."

Still triumphant and exultant, Elijah turned to Ahab and said, "Ride for your life before a downpour of rain makes the mud so deep that your chariot wheels will sink up to the hubs." Elijah girded his loins and ran before the chariot of Ahab into the city of Samaria. The old prophet thought he would be hailed as a great conqueror. Instead, Jezebel leaned out of the window and told him that she, personally, would see that he was beheaded before that same time tomorrow. Elijah fled to the deep forest and sat under a juniper tree. Life just didn't make sense.

I am sure something like this was in the minds of Jesus' disciples in the garden of Gethsemane when he told Simon Peter to put up his sword. He said to Peter and to the others, "Do you not know that I can call down a legion of angels if I need them?"

And throughout the trial, and then the torture of the crucifixion, I am sure they reasoned something like this: "He

had power over the sea to calm it with just a word. He raised
Lazarus from the dead after he had been in the tomb several
days. He healed every leper that he met. He restored sight
to the blind. Why did he let this happen to himself? He
said he could call down a legion of angels—why, why, why
didn't he?"

It just didn't make sense that he would let them scourge
him until his back was a gory mess; spit in his face; place
a crown of thorns on his head and press it down until the
blood ran down his face; and then crucify him. Is there an
answer to all these seemingly insensible things? The answer
is in four parts.

First, throughout the Bible we find many statements that
are varied in their expression but carry the same great message: *Since this world belongs to God, he is under no obliga-
tion to explain to us what happens.* God made it. God rules it.
God will destroy it when he is ready, and there isn't one thing
we can do about it. With our little finite minds, we grow
rebellious and say, "It doesn't make sense." And we forget
the words of God in Isaiah: "My thoughts are not your
thoughts, neither are your ways my ways. . . . For as the
heavens are higher than the earth, so are my ways higher
than your ways, and my thoughts than your thoughts" (Isa.
55:8–9).

Likewise in the book of Jeremiah, God reminds the grand
old prophet of this very fact. Jeremiah was arrogant enough
to argue with God about something that he couldn't understand. He said:

Let me talk with thee of thy judgments: Wherefore doth the
way of the wicked prosper? Wherefore are all they happy that
deal very treacherously? Thou hast planted them, yea, they have
taken root: they grow, yea, they bring forth fruit: thou art near
in their mouth, and far from their reins. But thou, O Lord,

knowest me: thou hast seen me, and tried mine heart toward thee: pull them out like sheep for the slaughter, and prepare them for the day of slaughter (Jer. 12:1–3).

God might have answered Jeremiah with the same words quoted above from Isaiah. Instead, he pointed out to Jeremiah that his reasoning was all but ridiculous. His answer was: "If thou hast run with the footmen, and they have wearied thee, then how canst thou contend with horses? and if in the land of peace, wherein thou trustedst, they wearied thee, then how wilt thou do in the swelling of Jordan?" (Jer. 12:5).

In plain language he was saying, "You are fretting about a very little thing. You must learn to accept my commands without questioning. There are far bigger problems in front of us all, and far more important things with which you will have to deal. You see only a little part. I am looking at the whole."

Paul saw this when he wrote: "For we know in part, and we prophesy in part. But when that which is perfect is come, then that which is in part shall be done away. . . . For now we see through a glass, darkly; but then face to face: now I know in part; but then shall I know even as also I am known" (1 Cor. 13:9–12).

David said that we are strangers and sojourners. He realized that we live in this world by the sufferance of God. The world does not belong to us. We have no authority to say this must be or that must be. Very clearly, God says, "Thus far and no farther." When we cannot find an explanation for a thing that seems senseless, we need a faith that is strong enough to say with Paul, "All things work together for good to them that love God, to them who are called according to his purpose" (Rom. 8:28).

Here is where we need the faith and the trust that God
in his Word demands of us, if we would be his children and
do his work. We need a faith strong enough to say the words
of that grand old song by John H. Newman:

> Lead, kindly Light! amid th'encircling gloom,
>   Lead Thou me on;
> The night is dark, and I am far from home,
>   Lead Thou me on;
> Keep Thou my feet; I do not ask to see
> The distant scene; one step enough for me.

We need to appropriate the words of Jesus to his disciples in
that memorable fourteenth chapter of John, "Let not your
heart be troubled: ye believe in God." So God lays down a
roadblock and asks us to have faith, even though we cannot
understand.

The second answer is that full many a time wonderful
things happen to us that we do not deserve, and we drop
down humbly on our knees and thank God for being so good
to us. We tell him gratefully that it just doesn't make sense
that all of these marvelous things have come to us when we
are so undeserving and fail him so often. For a long time on
television a series of stories has run under the title "The Mil-
lionaire." Without a single exception, the recipients of the
million dollar certified checks have expressed their astonishment and amazement and have said in so many words, "This
just doesn't make sense."

The third answer has an appealing note. David expressed
it when he asked in awe and wonder, "What is man, that
thou art mindful of him?" Jesus told us the hairs of our
heads are numbered and that God sees the sparrow that falls.
He told us of the shepherd that went looking for one sheep.
It is wonderful that God, who is as high above us as the heav-

ens are above the earth, would come and be closer to us than our dearest friend. To us he gives that sweet assurance that he hears every prayer and that, where two or three are gathered together in his name, he is there.

When we look at all of these things, we realize that we have no ground on which to stand and defiantly say that something awful which has happened to us doesn't make sense.

The fourth answer is that time often reveals to us that the thing we thought didn't make sense was an integral part of God's beautiful plan. Dr. J. N. Barnette, speaking at Ridgecrest Assembly one year, told us of a sixteen-year-old girl who wrote to Mr. Willard K. Weeks asking him to please let her be on the staff for the summer. In reply, he told her she must wait until she was eighteen. Another letter came the next year reminding Mr. Weeks that she would be eighteen the following summer and that she was anxious that he save a place for her. In due time, after her fourth letter to Mr. Weeks, he told her that he would be delighted to have her on the staff that summer.

Finally, she arrived, starry-eyed with happy anticipation of spending a glorious summer at Ridgecrest. But after two weeks, she came to Mr. Weeks's office to astonish him with the statement that she couldn't stay any longer.

"This doesn't make sense," he said. "What in the world has happened?"

Through the tears that she tried to keep back, she explained, "A few months ago, my family bought a home in the suburbs at the end of the car line. Every Sunday morning, when I went out to take the trolley to Sunday school, I saw a crowd of children playing in the streets. I realized there was no Sunday school close enough for them to attend, and their parents were too busy to take them into town. I am going back and organize a Sunday school in my own big home. I have no right to stay here enjoying all of these good things and leave them so neglected."

Dr. Barnette held up his hand and said, "Now, listen. At this very minute a church is going up in that neighborhood as the result of that young lady's sacrifice.' Time often reveals that the things that at first don't make sense finally become beautifully clear to us.

What are you doing about your roadblock?

8
What Do You Weigh?

On the front page of a newspaper some time ago appeared a most attractive pen picture. It was an old-fashioned set of balances, or scales. In the weighing pan on one side was a picture of a very fat sultan of an Oriental country. His head was adorned with a silk turban, and a happy smile wreathed his face. On the opposite side of the scale was a mountain of diamonds. The article below, describing the sultan's anniversary, said that his people had given him his weight in diamonds as a present. Since he weighed 264 pounds, you can only guess at the value of that huge pile of diamonds. The figures must have been staggering.

As I sat there looking at it, two passages of Scripture came immediately to mind. I am pretty sure that you will remember the first passage. I shall just mention it in passing.

Belshazzar gave a great feast. Before the astonished eyes of his guests, a part of a hand came out from nowhere and wrote on the wall four words: "Mene, Mene, Tekel, Upharsin." Daniel interpreted the word "Tekel" to mean, "Thou art weighed in the balances, and art found wanting."

The other verse, in Job 31:6, is the one that is filled with such a great message for us: "Let me be weighed in an even balance, that God may know mine integrity." Job was talking to his so-called comforters. They had been interpreting his disasters as the result of his disobedience and sins. His defense was this magnificent statement: "Let God weigh me in

59

an even balance [that is, in scales that are perfectly balanced], and both you and God can examine my integrity."

The picture in the newspaper and this reply bring to my mind three sets of balances that it would be well for us to keep in mind always:

First, what do you weigh in your own scales? This set is individual and belongs to you alone. No one can see the face of it except you. There are many things about you that no one else knows. You know yourself better than anyone else in the world knows you. What do you weigh in your own little private set of scales?

Paul said, "Let a man examine himself." What are the desires of your heart? What are the things for which you yearn earnestly? Are they beautiful things, high things, the "exceeding things" as Paul called them? To what do you aspire? What is the purpose of your life? What kind of pictures do you hang on the walls of your imagination? Are they ugly, vulgar pictures; or is your mind continually filled with pure, lovely thoughts and wishes?

One of my fellow pastors said, "My wife and I took into our home for a few weeks a young lady who had just come to work in a big department store. She had financial troubles, and we were trying to help her temporarily. We were greatly concerned to find that she stored up in her mind all of the slights and grievances of the day.

"When we sat down to the evening meal every night, she unloaded them on us. Her eyes flashed with anger and defiance and self-pity. Her determination to get even and hit back was written on her face and between the lines of her conversation. She little realized that she was weaving the warp and the woof of her character. The proverb came back to us, 'As [a man] thinketh in his heart, so is he.' "

What you weigh in your own scales is most important.

It can bring you happiness and exhilaration. It can add a lilt to life and help you face the dawn of a new day with joy and confidence. On the other hand, it can make you feel unworthy, unclean, and not fit to live. Let me illustrate.

I had finished the sermon one night in Dr. R. G. Lee's church in Memphis. As the crowd thinned out around the pulpit, Dr. Frank S. Groner came up to me and, smiling, said, "Come over to the Baptist Memorial Hospital while you are here. We want to examine your head."

I answered jestingly, "Was the sermon that bad?"

As we laughed together, he said, "Seriously, Dr. Strain wants to give you a physical, and he wants to make especially sure the skull fracture that you received in that automobile accident is completely healed." I told him to thank Dr. Strain most graciously for me and to tell him that I would be there the next day.

Several days later, after all of the tests had been made, I went back to Dr. Strain's office to see the reports. I had to wait in the outer office for half an hour. Then Dr. Strain opened his office door and followed a miserable-looking man out into the waiting room. He stood watching the man until he was out of sight, and then he beckoned to me.

As I sat down in his office, the worried look was still on his face. After a moment of silence, he said, "Dr. Angell, the man who just left this office is going to kill himself. I have been talking to him for an hour. When I felt I couldn't change his mind, I told him that you were sitting out there and that I would like so much to let him tell his troubles to you. His answer was, 'No, I'm too rotten to live. The things I have done are inexcusable and horrible. I deserve to die, and I am going to die today. The whole world will be better off when I am dead.' "

I repeat, what you weigh in your own scales is a matter of

vast importance. It can mean the difference between life
and death. It can mean having the abundant life that Jesus
told us about, or it can mean a miserable existence and even
death.

Then, what do you weigh in the scales of others? These are
scales that *you* cannot see. They are turned the other way.
We are all familiar with that little sentence, "O wad some
power the giftie gie us to see oursels as ithers see us!"

These scales are more important than we sometimes think.
Influence is sacred. No Christian has the right to say, "I
don't care what people think of me." Paul realized the importance of it when he said, "Adorn the doctrine [gospel]."
He knew the importance of making the Christian life so
beautiful that others would want what you have.

"What do you weigh in the scales of other people?" is a
searching question. Are people better because of your life?
Are they better because they know you? Are people glad
when you walk into a room? Are you greeted with smiles
or does a silence fall over those gathered there?

When Millard Jenkins was pastor of the First Baptist
Church in Abilene, Texas, I went to help him in a revival
service. One day he and I went down to a big garage to see
a mechanic who was not a Christian. His wife and children
were members of the church. This young mechanic hadn't
missed a single night of the meeting. We found the owner of
the garage in the office out front. He was a dedicated Christian. Dr. Jenkins asked him if we might stop one of his
mechanics from work long enough to talk to him about his
spiritual life.

To our surprise, this big Christian owner of the garage
shook his head in the negative and, smiling broadly, said,
"I am afraid I can't disturb him right now. In fact, I think
you are too late."

I was so astonished at this, I immediately asked, "Why?"

Still smiling he said, "Well, just step up on that chair outside the door and look over the tops of those cars, and you will see two men standing near the far corner of the garage."

Dr. Jenkins immediately stepped up on the chair and then with a low whistle said, as if talking to himself, "The mayor of Abilene is talking to the man we came to see."

"Fifteen minutes ago," said the manager, "the mayor came in and gravely asked me if he could pay the salary of that young man for half an hour, for he wanted to talk to him about his Saviour. I told him firmly, 'No, you cannot pay me anything, but you can go back there and talk to him just as long as you want to and tell him, for me, that he can have the whole afternoon off if he wants to talk to you about his salvation.'" Turning to me, he continued, "The mayor lives his religion. He doesn't have to make any apologies, and there is no embarrassment when he goes to talk to someone about Christianity. Everybody in the city knows that he tries to live just like his Lord wants him to live."

What a wonderful thing it would be if all of us who profess the name of Jesus would weigh as much as that mayor in the scales of others.

Finally, what do we weigh in the scales of God? These are the scales about which Job is talking. His desire was that God would weigh him in an even balance so that God might know his integrity. I wonder if all of us could pray Job's prayer, or wish Job's wish, that God would weigh us in *his* scales. How many of us would want the people we know to look at God's scales when we are put in that even balance? If God were to put us in his balances today and on the other side place what he expects us to be, and what we should be, how would the balances stand? Would there still be an even balance?

Of course, God's scales do not weigh avoirdupois, and Job

was not talking about either avoirdupois weight or troy weight. He was talking about those scales of God which weigh the intangible things, the invisible things. God's scales do weigh such things as integrity, courage, zeal for the kingdom work, honesty, sincerity, earnestness, and especially faith.

One of the best illustrations of the kind of faith we ought to have was an experience that I had at Paisano. Dr. George W. Truett was on the other side of the world one summer, and I was preaching in his place at the Paisano Encampment in Texas. They had a unique custom of charging no one for meals throughout the ten days of that assembly. The meals were cooked in big, ranch chuck wagons and served cafeteria style.

On the last Sunday they took up an offering at the morning service for the next year. For twenty-five years, Dr. Truett had taken this offering; and, of course, nobody could take an offering like Dr. Truett. The offerings had always been sufficient to finance the next year's encampment. On Saturday, a group of us, who had charge of the program for the year, met Brother Mike Milligan, God's missionary to the cowboys, whose vision and labor had established this encampment. Since I was preaching in Dr. Truett's place, they assigned me this tremendous task. My faith wasn't strong enough to think I could do it like it ought to be done.

Saturday night came, and I prayed and wept a little as I asked God to please give me some extra help on the morrow. Early the next morning, I went over to see Brother Milligan. Paisano Encampment had been his dream, and he and God had brought it to pass. A thousand acres of land and a herd of cattle had been donated by the ranchers.

Mr. Milligan was growing old and getting very feeble. He had a long white beard and looked like the picture I have always had of Moses. He always sat down close to the pulpit in a chair covered with calfskin. Since he was losing his hearing, he cupped his hands behind his ears when I preached. His faith was as strong as the Rock of Gibraltar.

I sat down in front of him that morning and said, "Brother Milligan, all of us are deeply concerned about the offering today. The others have asked me to take it, but I think you ought to take it. These people will do anything you want them to do. They all love you, and everybody knows the great sacrifices you have made to preach the gospel of Jesus Christ to the cowboys."

He asked with a smile, "Are you afraid?"

And I said, "Yes, sir, we are all afraid."

Still smiling he said, "Stop worrying. This is God's work, and he will take care of it. Last night I got down on my knees, and I told God, 'You know Dr. Truett is not here, and you know you have only a few wonderful servants like Dr. Truett. Now, help Roy Angell tomorrow morning to take that offering.' "

He continued, "Before I got my clothes on this morning, there came a knock at the door. I opened it, and Mr. Kokernot [the wealthiest ranch owner there and a deacon in the First Baptist Church of San Antonio, beloved by all of us] was standing there with a check in his hand. He told me that he had just received a message from his ranch and that he would have to leave immediately. He handed me a check for one thousand dollars to put into the offering, and then he said, 'We want to send Dr. Truett a cablegram and tell him we have more than enough money in the bank for the next assembly. So here is a blank check with my name signed to it. When you count the offering, fill in the amount that we need so we can send him the message that the offering was more than sufficient.' "

9
"How Readest Thou?"

In the law of Moses there were 613 commandments for the guidance of behavior, all the way from important things like putting God first to unimportant things like the kind of food one was to eat; consequently, there was a running argument among the teachers of the law as to what was most important. One day one of these teachers heard Jesus answering certain questions of his enemies. He liked the way Jesus went about it, and since he thought he might get some light on this old debate, he asked, "Which is the first commandment of all?"

Jesus' answer has become a classic. His incisive intellect cut through the maze of the 613 rules, and he picked out two. "The first of all the commandments is, Hear, O Israel; the Lord our God is one Lord: And thou shalt love the Lord thy God with all thy heart, and with all thy soul, and with all thy mind, and with all thy strength: . . . And the second is like, namely this, Thou shalt love thy neighbor as thyself" (Mark 12:29-30) . It must have made a deep impression on his hearers, for a little while later a lawyer quoted it word for word. Luke records it in the tenth chapter of his Gospel: "a certain lawyer stood up, and tempted him saying, Master, what shall I do to inherit eternal life?" Jesus, realizing it was a temptation and not a sincere question, did not answer him as he answered the scribe, but asked him in turn, "What is written in the law? How readest thou?" It was there the lawyer quoted him. I think that Jesus put the emphasis on the word *"thou,"* and it is a good question for us to ponder.

Three occasions recently have brought this question very much to my mind. The first was a story that Dr. John A. Redhead, Jr. told of an unlettered preacher. This old preacher always spoke against higher education; and when someone asked him why he did not believe in going to college, he said his Bible backed him up. When he was asked further for a particular reference, he quoted the statement of Jesus: "In such an hour as ye *think not* the Son of man cometh." His argument went like this: colleges teach you to *think,* and *thinking* is an obstacle to the return of Christ; therefore, college education is wrong. Of course, the poor man misunderstood entirely the words of Jesus, *"How readest thou?".*

Second, two nice looking young men came to my study and said to me, "We have just come to the city, and we are looking for a church." You can imagine with what a happy smile I welcomed them and told them they had already found the best church in this part of the world. Then I asked them to be seated. One of them began the conversation by saying, "First, we have to ask you a question. What do you believe about the millennium? Are you a postmillennialist or a premillennialist?" The question both surprised and shocked me. Actually, it irritated me a little. After waiting a good half-minute, I finally asked them, "Do you consider that the most important question about a church and its minister?" Without a moment's hesitation they answered, "It's the most important question in the Bible." Immediately there came to my mind the Master's question to the lawyer, "How readest thou?"

The third incident was when Dr. W. W. Adams, professor at the Southern Baptist Theological Seminary, brought the devotions for our Florida State Convention a while ago. Every one of us felt that we had never heard a finer series of messages. We deeply appreciated his sense of humor as well as his exegesis. In one message, he told this story on himself; in substance he said: "A student registered for one of my classes and came the first day. I didn't see him again for about a week, and then he never did attend another class. Class attendance was not compulsory, but in order to pass the course the students were required to attend more than half of the sessions. After about a month I marked his name off of the roll. At the end of the semester, to my surprise, I found his paper among the others of those who had taken the examination. My associate took part of the papers, and I took part of them, to read and grade. A few days later my associate brought this young man's paper to me with a grade of 99 on it. I was dumfounded. Since neither of us could remember ever having seen him, I sent my assistant to find him and bring him to the office. When he came in very humbly and quietly, I said to him, 'You had no right to take this examination. You didn't attend classes.'

"He answered, 'Oh, I'm sorry. I didn't know I had to attend.'

" ' Look at this grade of 99 and explain it.'

"He shifted from one foot to the other and, blushing a little, answered, 'Doctor, I did attend two classes, but I got awfully confused; otherwise, I would have made 100.' " Dr. Adams went on to say that some people read the Bible like that. They let it drop open and read a few verses, and a week later they let it drop open at some other place and read a few verses. Then they go away and say that when they read the Bible they get confused. "How readest thou"—God's Word?

How readest thou the attributes of God? You remember that, when Uzziah died, Isaiah said: "I saw also the Lord sitting upon a throne, high and lifted up, and his train filled the

temple" (Isa. 6:1). Isaiah fell on his face in awe and reverence. Somehow, through the years, we have lost this attitude
toward God. Many of us have ceased to realize the power and
authority of God. Maybe we have rationalized about God.
Certainly, in many of our church services there is anything
but a spirit of reverence and awe. Have we forgotten that
we come to church to sit for a little while, in a special way,
in the presence of God?

It always hurts me to hear someone, while praying, use
the word "you" in addressing God. It sounds too familiar. It is
certainly out of step with this picture of Isaiah down on his
face saying, "Woe is me! for I am undone; . . . mine eyes
have seen the King, the Lord of hosts" (Isa. 6:5). Or we
might remember old Simon Peter, kneeling in a boat half
filled with fish and water, with his arms around the knees of
Jesus and his heart crying out in despair, "Depart from me;
for I am a sinful man, O Lord."

Sherwood Eddy made this great truth live when he told of
the visit of Miss Amy Carmichael to his church. Miss Carmichael was a missionary to the Far East. She was home on fur-
lough and had thrilled a big audience with her experience in
establishing an orphanage in that part of the world. When
she had finished and taken her seat, the pastor asked, "Would
anyone like to ask Miss Carmichael a question?" Sherwood
Eddy said, "There was half a minute of silence, and then I
asked, 'Miss Carmichael, would you tell us how you became
a missionary?'

"Smiling, Miss Carmichael walked to the front of the pulpit again and told us this thrilling story. 'I was reared in the
country and didn't have much chance for an education. While
I was just a girl, God laid it on my heart to want to be a
missionary. I talked to everybody about it. I prayed about
it, but no one encouraged me. They couldn't see, and I

couldn't see, how I could ever get get enough education to be
a missionary. I finally became discouraged and decided it was
no use for me to keep on wishing and praying, for it was just
impossible. Then, one night in prayer meeting, I sat in my
usual seat just behind the grandest Christian deacon I ever
knew. His prayers always moved me deeply. His life was so
wholesome and his countenance so benign that he lifted
everyone around him. This particular night the pastor called
on him to pray. He began his prayer, as usual, by thanking
God for many things. From there his prayer went into peti-
tions, and he closed it in an unusual way.

" 'I can still hear his words, "We ask thee for all of these
things because we know that thou canst do . . . [there was
a long silence; he didn't seem to know how to finish that
prayer] thou canst do . . . *anything.*" Suddenly my spirits
soared. I felt that God was talking to me, and I repeated that
last sentence of his prayer, "Thou canst do anything, Lord.
Please make me a missionary." ' Miss Carmichael's voice
choked up, and she ended the answer to my request with
'that's how I became a missionary.' "

Next, how readest thou what the Scriptures say about the
kingdom of God? Have you ever noticed how often Jesus
referred to the kingdom as something wonderful and much
to be desired? He spoke of it as a treasure hidden in a field,
as a great pearl, as a beautiful vineyard with wine press and
tower, as a gala wedding, and, most important of all, as a
feast. I am afraid we have neglected this view of the kingdom.
I am afraid that too often we have spoken of it in terms of
sacrifice, suffering, and trials. We hear a lot about the cost
of being a Christian and the price of stewardship. While
these things are true, we have misread God's Word if we fail
to see that being a Christian is about the most glorious thing
God ever gave us the privilege of becoming. To be sure, the

kingdom of God is a feast, and we should always think of it as something marvelous and wonderful. But we should never forget that the people who come to this feast usually are *invited to it by the servants of the Lord.* Paul called himself a servant. Jesus put the emphasis on being a servant on the last night he lived on earth as a man. He girded himself with a towel and washed the feet of his disciples.

Once Jesus told a story about a man who prepared a feast and invited many people to come. But all who were invited began to make excuses and didn't come. I suppose that every one of us ministers has preached about that story and done just as I have done—put the emphasis on the excuses.

I read the story recently and realized I had missed one of its great messages. The people who were invited were invited by a *servant.* Five times the word "servant" occurs in that brief parable. It was the servant that was sent to remind them of the feast. It was the servant that came back to the master with the sad news that they were not coming. It was the servant that went out to the streets and the lanes of the city and brought in the poor and the maimed and the halt and the blind. It was the servant who told his lord that there was yet room, and again it was the servant that went into the highways and hedges for others. There would have been no feast without the servant, nor will the kingdom of God be a feast for the sinners of this world without a servant. We Christians are commissioned and commanded to be those servants of the Lord.

Third, how readest thou the story of redemption? Is it only a story of salvation for eternity? Is it only a story of salvation for our souls? Do we put the words "redemption" and "heaven" so close together that we leave out the Master's words about "abundant life" here on earth? We are not redeemed only to have our names written on the scrolls of heaven. When we are redeemed, we are ushered into a new life on earth, and God sets before us an open door to beautiful living. As Paul said, "Old things are passed away; behold all things are become new."

Roger Babson illustrated it with this true incident. He said: "I went over to see one of the finest men that ever lived on this earth. I spent most of the day with him. We became very confidential late in the afternoon, and finally he said to me, 'I want to show you something that I have never shown to anyone.' He took me into a large, spacious room in his house. As he unlocked the door, he said, 'You are the first man I have brought to this room in ten years.' Naturally, my curiosity was on edge. He took me by the arm, walked me slowly to the center of the room, and stood facing an oil painting—a perfect likeness of my host.

"I exclaimed to him, 'That's a good picture! It looks exactly like you.'

"He turned his face toward me, and it literally beamed, 'Tell me the truth, please,' he said, 'does it really look like me?'

"I looked at it again and said, 'It's as fine a likeness as I have ever seen of anybody.'

"Then he surprised me again as he murmured, 'I have a notion to get down on my knees and say my prayers.' Naturally, I wanted to know why he felt that way. Then he told me this astounding story: 'One day the roof fell in on me financially. I was ready to destroy myself. A few days later an old friend, a portrait painter, invited me to lunch with him. I was so depressed I told him I would go some other time, if he would give me a rain check, because today I wasn't good company. But he insisted, and as we ate I was conscious of his close scrutiny. Finally, I asked him, a bit irritably, why he was staring at me so. Slowly and quietly, he answered, "I would like to paint your portrait." I demurred, but when he insisted so strongly, I finally agreed. He wouldn't let me look at it until he had finished; then, before he took the cover off, he made a little speech. "I have painted what I see in you, not just your face, but your real self, your real heart and personality."

" 'When I did look at it, I protested, "I'm not like that. That is not the face I see in my mirror." Many, many times I have stood here and prayed to my Heavenly Father to bring out the best that was in me. Today, you tell me it is a good likeness. Today, I realize redemption is not just for the soul; it is in part for here and now. I think of those words Jesus spoke to Simon Bar-jona, "Thou art Peter." Jesus changed him and me, too.' "

10
Consider Christ

When John Quincy Adams was President of the United States, he did a dramatic thing. He called both Houses of Congress together for a special meeting. He walked upon the rostrum carrying two bushel measures. Holding one in each hand, he said to the audience, "The bushel measure in my right hand came from South Carolina; the one in my left hand comes from the city of New York. One of these bushel measures contains sixty-eight cubic inches more than the other one." He stood silent for a few moments to let the implication sink in; then he slowly placed them side by side on the floor. In the same deliberate way, he walked over to a little table and picked up two one-pound weights, the kind that were used on a set of balance scales to weigh produce. With measured words he said, "This weight in my right hand came from Massachusetts; this other one came from Maine. One of them weighs nearly an ounce more than the other." Again he waited a few moments for everyone to grasp the problem. Then with a resonant voice he said, "Gentlemen, we need a standard measure and a standard weight for the United States of America."

Thus came into existence what is now known in Washington as the "House of Wonders." Officially, it is the Bureau of Weights and Measures. In it is a set of scales so delicate that the man who wishes to weigh something accurately must stand at least ten feet away from it lest the heat of his body upset the balance. I have read that the balance is so delicate that it could weigh a wisp of smoke. Also, there is an iron bar an inch square and a foot long, likewise so delicately balanced that it can compute the distance that a fly, lighting on one end of it, would move the needle.

We can readily see the importance of such standards for physical things, but do we realize how much more important it is that we have a norm, a standard, for our moral and spiritual lives? Isn't this what was in God's mind when he sent Jesus into our world to live and to teach? Jesus was forever correcting the standards of his time. He told his disciples to beware of the Pharisees, who thought that their piety was indicated by their long prayers and their public giving. Jesus told them that the Pharisees had already received their reward, for "when thou doest alms, let not thy left hand know what thy right hand doeth: . . . And when thou prayest, . . . enter into thy closet, and when thou hast shut thy door, pray to thy Father" (Matt. 6:3–6). Until Jesus came, the Pharisees, with their prayers and their gifts and their attitudes, formed the religious standards of the day.

Years later the writer of Hebrews, faced with the same basic problem under slightly different conditions, said, "For consider him [Christ] that endured such contradiction of sinners against himself, lest ye be wearied and faint in your minds. Ye have not yet resisted unto blood, striving against sin" (Heb. 12:3–4). He was saying that Christ is the norm and standard for all things in a Christian's life. Look briefly at two realms where we modern people need so much to keep Christ as our pattern.

First, Christ is our norm for what God expects of us. It was brought out in Jesus' life by his enemies in a most carefully laid plan. A man came up to Jesus and, I think, spoke in a most gracious way, "Master, thou art a very wise teacher.

Thou understandest everything. Please tell us, is it right for us to pay tribute to Caesar?" Jesus saw through his assumed graciousness and knew that, if he said yes, all of the crowd that was gathered around would boo him and lose confidence in his teachings. The one thing that aggravated them most was the tribute that Caesar exacted, and the people they despised the most were the tax collectors. Jesus knew also that, if he answered no, immediately the Pharisees would run to Pilate and tell him that Jesus was a rebel and was advising people not to pay tribute to Caesar.

I have always thought there was a smile on Jesus' face as he asked the young man for a coin. Then, after turning it over a few times in his hand, he said to the young man, "There is an inscription on this coin. Whose is it?" When the young man answered, "It is Caesar's," still smiling, Jesus handed it back to him and said those unforgettable words, "Render unto Cacsar the things that are Caesar's and render unto God the things that are God's." Jesus literally did both of these things. He once said to Simon Peter, "Go catch a fish, and in his mouth you will find a coin. Use it to pay our taxes." On the other hand, he spent his whole life rendering to his Heavenly Father the things that belonged to him— namely, allegiance, reverence, and obedience. There often fell from his lips such sentences as "I must do the will of him that sent me" and "not my will but thine be done." When the disciples begged him not to go up to Jerusalem, he gravely answered, "I must," and the record reads that "he steadfastly set his face to go to Jerusalem."

In the second chapter of Acts, you can see in his disciples the same *abandon* that was in the life of Christ. When the multitudes heard the disciples in Jerusalem speaking the languages of the Parthians, Medes, Asia, and of many other nations, they mockingly accused them of being drunk. They could not find any other explanation for their daring. These disciples were acting as if they were not afraid of reprisals; their actions were uninhibited. There was in their attitude a sense of well-being. And they appeared to feel that their audience would agree with them and approve of what they were saying, just as so often a man who has had a few drinks is in a good humor with the world and thinks that everybody likes him just as he likes everybody else.

Twice in my life I have met John Tyler, the man who spent his last years going from city to city to speak wherever opportunity offered, both from the pulpit and in the streets, about the terribleness of liquor. One day in my study at Baton Rouge, I read to him this passage in the second chapter of Acts and asked if there was any similarity between the two.

His face lighted up as he answered, "We have a word from the Greeks, 'euphoria,' which literally means a sense of well-being, or extreme exuberance. I ran through two fortunes— one left me by my grandfather, one by my father. I literally drank them up. I was a disgrace to my family, and they disowned me. They demanded that I stay away from home. I was so miserable that I had to do something to make me forget. Two small drinks of liquor were enough; then I had a sense of well-being. I liked everybody, and I imagined everybody liked me. This was a false euphoria.

"Now, when these disciples were filled with the Holy Spirit, they had the real euphoria. They *were* exuberant and fearless. They just didn't care what happened to them, so they openly accused the rulers of the synagogue and the Pharisees of crucifying God's own Son. Read the last three verses in the same chapter, '[They] sold their possessions and goods, and parted them to all men, as every man had need. And they, continuing daily with one accord in the temple,

and breaking bread from house to house, did eat their meat
with gladness and singleness of heart, Praising God, and having favour with all the people. And the Lord added to the
church daily such as should be saved' " (Acts 2:45–47).

I think God expects something like that of us. Certainly,
the world needs to see in Christian people, not long, serious
faces, but lives that are filled with exuberance and enthusiasm for the Christian way of living. We should be the most
joyous and the happiest people on earth. God expects us to
live our Christianity in such a beautiful way that it will be
contagious. He expects us to live it in such a way that others
will want what we have. Indeed, Jesus and those disciples are
a splendid measuring rod for what God expects of us.

Second, Christ is our norm for what we can expect of God.
In many places, Jesus told his disciples and us what we could
expect of his Heavenly Father, of him, and of the Comforter
that God promised to send. He told them to ask and expect
an answer. He told them to go and expect his presence to be
with them. He told them to expect his Spirit to guide them.
He told them to forgive and expect to be forgiven.

Maybe the most beautiful passage in the New Testament is
the fifteenth chapter of Luke. In it Jesus illustrates what we
can expect of God when we have done wrong or made a mistake. It seems to me that God said, "Luke, record these para-
bles carefully, very carefully. Show that Jesus said the same
thing three times. Tell the whole world that a woman lost a
coin that was very precious to her, that she moved out everything in the house, and that she got her broom and frantically
swept it clean until she found that coin. Then tell how she
called her neighbors to come and rejoice with her because the
precious coin was found.

"Tell the whole world that a sheep strayed away from the
flock and was left behind when the shepherd led the rest of

them back to the fold. When the shepherd counted them, he found ninety-nine safe, but one was still out in the mountains, lost. Without a moment's hesitation, he took a bottle of water, some food, and his shepherd's crook and went back into the mountains to find that one lost sheep. 'And when he cometh home, he calleth together his friends and neighbours, saying unto them, Rejoice with me; for I have found my sheep which was lost. I say unto you, that likewise joy shall be in heaven over one sinner that repenteth, more than over ninety and nine just persons, which need no repentance' (Luke 15:6–7).

"Tell the whole world that a father had two sons and that one of them went astray. He did everything that he shouldn't have done. He disgraced his father's name, he wasted his substance, and threw away years of his own life. Paint the scene of his return so graphically that 'he who runs may read.' The old father ran to meet him, didn't even listen to the boy's apologies, but yelled to the servants, 'Bring a robe, a ring, and sandals. Then prepare a royal feast and invite all of the neighbors to come and rejoice.' "

In simple language, we can expect God to do just what Jesus did on the cross—forgive.

Dr. Charles Crowe illustrated this splendidly. In substance he said, "I was a chaplain in the last war and was invalided back to the hospital. For quite a while, I was blind. When I did get my sight back, I found I was in a hospital room with about forty other soldiers. It was a real treat to look around and see everybody, especially the visitors who were bringing flowers and candy and other nice things to eat. Opposite my bed across the aisle was a bed with a screen around it and a small sign which I couldn't read from my bed. I saw the visitors stop and read it and pass on. When finally I could get up and limp around a little, I went across the aisle and read the notice, which said "Positively No Visitors by Order of the Colonel."

Chaplain Crowe continued, "I looked up and down the room to see if anyone was watching me. There was not a nurse in sight, so I pushed the screen away a little and stepped inside. The boy in the bed looked up startled and blurted out, 'Don't you know that nobody is allowed in here?'

"I said, 'Yes, I read the sign. What's the matter? What did you do?'

"With a sigh, he answered, 'Well, it's no secret. There is no reason why I shouldn't tell you. When I was in the front trench, the boys on both sides of me were shot down, and I got scared. I knew if I ran they would court-martial me, so I put a sand bag over my foot to cover the powder burns and shot myself. But they found it out, and now I am in disgrace. When I am well enough, I will be court-martialed, and I reckon I will be put to death.' When I told him I was a chaplain, he sat up and said, 'Well, you are the very man I want to talk to. I know I shouldn't have done it. I know I will have to pay the penalty for it, but I want to know if God can forgive a thing like this.' "

Charles Crowe said, "I got my Bible and read to him the fifteenth chapter of Luke; then I read the words of Jesus from the cross 'Father, forgive them; for they know not what they do.' I told him of the many times that the children of Israel had sinned and of the many times that God forgave them. I read him Simon Peter's question to Jesus, 'Shall we forgive our brother seven times?' and how Jesus answered that he should forgive him not just seven times but seventy times seven.

"I left him smiling and went back to my bed.

"In a few days, the Colonel came, pushed aside the screen, and talked with the boy for half an hour. When he came out, he called the nurse and said, 'Take these screens down by my order.'

"I was waiting for the Colonel to come out, and I asked, 'May I be his advocate when the court-martial comes up?'

"The Colonel's voice was husky with emotion as he answered, 'There won't be any court-martial. I forgave him just like you told him his God would forgive.' "

Of course, there are a thousand other things that we can expect of God, but none of them so stirs and moves us as this one in which we see plainly God's love and forgiveness.

11
What God Hath Joined Together

Lacy palms, flickering candlelight, soft music, and a hushed air of expectancy filled our church auditorium. Once again I had repeated, almost automatically, the final words of the marriage ceremony, "What God hath joined together, let not man put asunder," to the fine young couple who stood before me pledging their love and devotion for life. As they knelt after the prayer, the soloist sang in a quiet, rich voice "The Lord's Prayer." It went just as usual until the singer came to the sentence "And forgive us our debts, as we forgive our debtors." This arrested my thoughts, and I suddenly realized that, since God had joined *these two things* together, man should not put them asunder.

My mind left the wedding scene and wandered to thoughts of many other things not in the wedding ceremony, things that God has joined together and that man has no right to tear asunder. I thought of God's words to Abraham: "I will bless thee, . . . and thou shalt be a blessing" (Gen. 12:2). And then there is *receiving* and *giving*. In Jesus' own words, "Give, and it shall be given unto you; . . . For with the same measure that ye mete withal it shall be measured to you again" (Luke 6:38). There are many others, but consider three of the most obvious.

First, look at *creed* and *conduct*. By "creed" I do not refer to the Apostles' Creed or any other one formally adopted by a convention. I mean our genuine belief in Jesus Christ and his way of life, our dedication to him and his teachings. A flock of questions come immediately to our minds: Does our conduct always reflect our creed? Do the people who know us best take knowledge that we have been with Jesus? Are the things we *do* consistent with the things we *profess?* Can we say with Paul, "I was not disobedient unto the heavenly vision," and, "For me to live is Christ"?

This was brought home to me by an article I read in one of our secular magazines. I emphasize that it was a *secular* magazine and not a Christian periodical. It deals mostly with drama, books, art, and music across the world. One of the editors had made a trip to Indonesia. There he met a Hindu priest who was very much interested in America and the American way of life. The priest invited him into his home. They sat down among the cushions and talked for hours. The editor finally asked the Hindu priest this personal question, "Are you happy in the work that you are doing, and are you doing the things that you most want to do?"

The answer was instantaneous: "No."

The American then asked, "What would you like to do?"

He was not ready for the Hindu's answer. The priest got up from the cushions and walked backward and forward across the room. Then he startled the American by saying, "I would like to be a missionary to America."

Surprised, the editor asked, "Do you mean you would like to go to America and try to get them to accept the Hindu religion? You mean you would like to try to convert them to your beliefs?"

Again the answer was an emphatic no! The Hindu continued, "I would like to be a missionary to America to take Christianity to the American people, I mean the kind of Christianity the missionaries have who come over here. They are so dedicated, loyal, and humble. They are enthusiastic and bubbling over with the great teachings of Jesus Christ, the most wonderful teachings ever given to man. I would like to go to your people and get them to take these teachings to heart and live them every day. Christianity has become a custom, and just a custom, to many of your countrymen. Thousands of businessmen and scientists come to my country every year. They are different from your missionaries. You can spend a week with one of them, and he will never mention his religion, never use the name of Christ, except in profanity." It is hard to read that without blushing.

Maybe we need to do what a crowd of men set out to do twenty years ago—rethink missions. But, above all, we need to keep our *creed* and our *conduct* in step. These are two things that God has joined together and, alas, we so easily and so freely tear apart.

Let us bring it a little closer home. A fellow pastor told me the secret of the faithfulness and usefulness of a family in his church. He said, "I had complimented the two of them on being so dependable and so dedicated. They looked at each other, and then the husband spoke: 'When we were first married, we were loyal Christians. We came to church regularly and made our religion a vital part of our home and our lives. Then into our home came our first baby. As soon as he was large enough, we brought him to the nursery. After he grew a little older, we found it easier just to drop him at Sunday school and then pick him up after Sunday school was over. This went on for several years. Then one Sunday morning at breakfast, after a long silence, our son asked, "Daddy, don't you love Jesus any more?"

" ' "Of course, I do," I answered. "What makes you ask that?"

" 'Timidly, he continued, "You never go to Sunday school with me. You just drop me off and then come back home. I just decided you didn't love him any more. And it upset me, because my teacher said that, if we love Jesus, we will do what he wants us to do. I try to do what he wants me to do."

"The father said, 'I reached over and covered that boy's hand with mine and said, "Sonny, I am ashamed of myself. I thought I had a lot of things that were more important, but I don't think I have. I'll be ready to go with you to Sunday school in just a few minutes. We are going in together as we used to do, and from now on I'm going every Sunday." ' "

That boy's question digs pretty deeply, and it's a good one for each of us to be asking ourselves: "Don't I love Jesus any more?" Are our *conduct* and our *creed* still joined together?

Next, man should not divorce *fellowship* and *service*. Our minds just naturally turn back to the words of the Great Commission "Ye shall be witnesses unto me"—beginning in Jerusalem. Think what would happen if the thousands of businessmen who go into the faraway places were all Christians of the first magnitude. Suppose on a Sunday they all crowded into the mission station closest to them, and the missionary, with a happy smile, could lay a hand on their shoulders and say, "I am glad you came. You bring strength with you. You can talk to these big businessmen in our community better than I can. Bring them to church with you next Sunday." Beloved, we could convert the world, and we would not need a Peace Corps. You think this is an impossible dream? This is exactly what communism is doing. Every businessman that goes out from Russia goes as a missionary for communism. In no time at all, they find the other Communists, and together they give half of their time and half of their income for the spread of communism.

When Dr. Roy McClain and I ate lunch together recently, he told me of a Communist that he had led to Christ. The Communist had some questions. "What part of my salary is

required?" Roy told him that we make no requirements, but
we hoped that everyone would be a tither. Then, as he is
able, he would make offerings as well. The Communist's
mouth dropped open. He said, "When you become a Communist, you are *required* to give one-half of your salary."
Then he asked, "What service is required of me?" Again the
Communist was surprised when he was told the things the
church hoped he would do. "Communism required every
one of us to give three hours a day, seven days a week" was
his response.

Have we watered down the obligations of Christianity?
Do we come to church as a matter of habit only to enjoy the
Christian fellowship? Have we forgotten that passage in Acts
2:44–47, which reads: "And all that believed were together,
. . . continuing daily with one accord in the temple, . . .
And the Lord added to the church daily such as should be
saved"? These disciples of Jesus used their fellowship to
strengthen themselves and to encourage one another, not as
an end in itself, but as a means to make them better witnesses.

Our Sunday school superintendent jarred all of us at a
Wednesday night supper for Sunday school officers and teachers. He very slowly made this statement that ended with a series of questions: "There is something I don't understand.
Our record on the board shows that you adults made 402 vis-
its last week, and it doesn't show a single new name added to
the roll. Whom did you visit? Did you just visit one another?
Didn't you visit one unsaved or unchurched person? Was it
just a social visit?"

Could this happen in your church? A minister, on vacation,
visited a fashionable church in one of our large cities. And
since he was on vacation, he was wearing casual clothes. Ar-
riving just before the service started, along with a number of

other people who were impressively dressed, he didn't receive much attention. The usher passed him in the foyer to bow to some richly dressed people and left him standing there while he, smiling and very courteous, ushered them up to choice seats. Then the usher came back and with no trace of a smile, in fact rather grudgingly and glumly, ushered him to a seat in the back. The minister then decided he would experiment a little. The next Sunday he dressed in his clerical best—long tails, striped trousers, and a big flower in his buttonhole. When he walked into the foyer of the church, this same usher, smiling graciously, ushered him up to the front this time and gave him a choice seat.

Are our churches a social fellowship instead of a place where we come to meet God and learn what he wants us to do for him? Do we come up to worship and then go out to serve? Hasn't God joined together *fellowship* and *service?* Jesus said, as he girded himself with a towel and washed the feet of the disciples, "The greatest of us shall be the servant of us all."

Finally, look at *conversion* and *confession.* Jesus emphasized repeatedly the danger of lighting a candle and putting it under a bushel. He emphasized the necessity of setting the candle in a candlestick where it would give light and where it would be seen of all men.

Clifton J. Allen, one of our finest Sunday school men, tells an interesting story about his father and uncle. They were small boys when their parents moved out West. They had lived there several years before the two boys were allowed to drive the wagon to the nearest town for supplies. One day they did not get started early enough, and on their way home a severe snowstorm overtook them just at dark. In a matter of minutes, they were lost. Since they were not dressed warmly enough for a blizzard, they would certainly freeze to death if they didn't find their way home soon. Their father anxiously went out to search for them, but he didn't dare go out of sight of the lights from the home lest he get lost. The mother put a light in every window and prayed earnestly to God to save her two boys.

Finally, one of the boys saw a faint light and used that as a guide to bring them to their own home. The next day their father cut down the tallest tree that he could handle; after trimming off the limbs, he made a light pole out of it and set it in the front yard. On its top he put a pulley with a rope attached. Every night he lighted a lantern and pulled it to the top of the pole so that it could act as a beacon to guide anyone who might be lost on the prairie.

Likewise, Jesus warned of the danger of trying to be a secret disciple. Clearly he said, "Whosoever therefore shall confess me before men, him will I confess also before my Father which is in heaven" (Matt. 10:32). The Philippian jailer, after the doors of the prison had been thrown open and yet no prisoner had escaped, asked Paul, "What must I do to be saved?" Paul told him to believe and be baptized. I am sure that Paul didn't mean all would have to be literally baptized to be saved but that the baptism was to be his public confession of his belief in Christ.

12
Living Carelessly

When World War I broke out, Dr. Cyrus Hamlin was a missionary in the Near East. He promptly volunteered to be an army chaplain and was gladly accepted because of his familiarity with the language and the people. The regiment to which he was assigned had a Turkish division. Dr. Hamlin and the Turkish colonel soon became good friends. The colonel regularly attended the chaplain's religious services, and they had many discussions about religion. One day, while they were in the chaplain's tent, the colonel said to him: "I like to hear you talk. You are good. Chaplain, if you could just show me one single piece of concrete proof that the Bible *is* the Word of God and I could accept it, it would ease something inside of me that just aches and aches and aches."

Dr. Hamlin reached for his Bible and started to turn the pages to find the thirteenth chapter of Isaiah. While looking, he asked, "Colonel, did you ever visit the ruins of Babylon?"

A sparkle came into the colonel's eyes, and his face lighted up as he answered quickly, "It is my choice hunting ground. It has been turned into a kind of park and is used by the Persian royalty as a hunting reserve." A smile came over his face as he continued: "A funny thing happened to me the last time I was there. Several of us employed an Arabian sheik to organize a safari. They were to look after our camp and prepare our meals. Early one morning we pitched our tents just inside of the old Babylon. Immediately we left for the day to hunt while all of the Arabs stayed behind to set up the camp. We returned a little before sunset to face a real surprise. The sheik and all of his Arabs were about to depart and leave us without any supper. Our protests were of no avail. I did my level best to get them to stay, but the sheik's answer was firm and positive.

" 'No, sir. No, sir. No Arabian spends the night in Babylon. For hundreds of years it has been a definitely observed custom.'

"Of course, I asked, 'Why?'

"His answer again surprised me: 'Babylon is haunted with ghosts and ghouls and goblins and satyrs. All kinds of weird noises and mysterious sounds come out of the caves of Babylon. We will be back in the morning, but we cannot spend the night.' We hunted for a week, and the Arabs left in the evening at sunset and came back in the morning at dawn." Dr. Hamlin said he guessed his mouth must have dropped open in astonishment, for the colonel said, "What's the matter with you?"

The chaplain handed the Bible to him and said, "Colonel, read this passage written by the prophet Isaiah: 'And Babylon, the glory of kingdoms, the beauty of the Chaldees' excellency, shall be as when God overthrew Sodom and Gomorrah. It shall never be inhabited, neither shall it be dwelt in from generation to generation: neither shall the Arabian pitch tent there; neither shall the shepherds make their fold there. But wild beasts of the desert shall lie there; and their houses shall be full of doleful creatures; and owls shall dwell there, and satyrs shall dance there. And the wild beasts of the islands shall cry in their desolate houses, and dragons in their pleasant palaces: and her time is near to come, and her days shall not be prolonged' " (Isa. 13:19–22).

When he had read it through, he shrugged his shoulders and said, "That's history."

Dr. Hamlin said, "You are wrong. You are dead wrong. That is not history; *that is prophecy*. That was written more than two hundred years before Babylon was destroyed. Isaiah had been dead more than two hundred years when Babylon fell. It is documented. We know exactly when Isaiah lived, and we know when Babylon was destroyed."

The colonel laid the Bible down and got up slowly from his seat. He paced silently backward and forward in the tent with a deep frown on his face. Finally, he stopped in front of Dr. Hamlin and said, "Say that over again, slowly." Dr. Hamlin repeated the statements and then read the passage of Isaiah to him again. With a voice that trembled a little, he said, "You shake my unbelief." And then with deep feeling he continued, "Chaplain, if I believed the Bible is the Word of God, I would use all of my wealth and fortune, and I would give every minute of my life, to take the story of your Jesus and your God to the people of the world."

The chaplain said, "The Turkish colonel had jarred me terribly. I wondered if God had used him for a whip. I hadn't been that dedicated and enthusiastic in taking the gospel to others. I realized *I hadn't cared that much* if my nation was in reality a Christian nation. And the Great Commission had not meant that much to me. I found myself saying to my Heavenly Father, 'O God, forgive me—please forgive me—for I haven't been the kind of a missionary or the kind of a chaplain or the kind of a Christian that you needed me to be. Forgive me, Father, please forgive me.' "

The words of the Turkish colonel were not just a whip for the chaplain. They are, indeed, a whip for every one of us. And when Isaiah takes up the story of Babylon again in the forty-seventh chapter, he writes one verse that we might well

read very profitably: "Therefore hear now this, thou that art
given to pleasures, that *dwellest carelessly,* that sayest in
thine heart, I am, and none else beside me" (Isa. 47:8).

We, like the Babylonians and the Chaldeans, have lived
carelessly and, as Isaiah meant, selfishly. We have been satisfied with making some little gift toward evangelism and missions. We believe the Bible is the Word of God, but very few
of us have ever shown the dedication that the Turkish colonel
felt would be the natural result of knowing that the Bible *is*
true, that it *is* God's Word, and that it *is* written to us. To be
sure, God doesn't want all of us to go as foreign missionaries,
but there is no excuse for neglecting the opportunities that
come to us daily for witnessing in the communities where we
live. The Great Commission does not read in Matthew 28:19
only that we should go and "teach all nations," but it also
reads in Acts 1:8, "Ye shall be witnesses unto me . . . [be-
ginning] in Jerusalem." Likewise, Jesus put the words in the
mouth of the man who made a great feast (the feast was a
symbol of the kingdom of God) and bade his servant to go
into the highways and hedges, to go into the streets and the
lanes, and compel the guests to come in.

The best illustration that I ever heard of what can be done
by one individual was given by Dr. John Timothy Stone, a
famous Presbyterian minister. One Monday morning, at the
General Ministers' Conference in Baltimore, the man who
was scheduled for the program of the day was taken ill and
could not be present. The president suggested that we use
the hour for testimonies, and he called on Dr. Stone because
we all liked to hear him speak and because he was considered
the outstanding preacher in Maryland. Without any apologies or any preliminary remarks, Dr. Stone began, "Yesterday was the red-letter day of my life. I have never been so
moved in all the days of my ministry. We had a Jewish-Ital-

ian boy to speak to our young people at the evening service. He had been converted recently, and he was on fire for Christ.

"He told the story of his conversion. 'I was on a soapbox in Times Square in New York, and I was enthusiastically belittling and low-rating America and Christianity. A man stopped to listen to me and then moved on around the circle, and I lost him in the crowd. When I had finished speaking, I found him standing beside me. There was an engaging smile on his face, as he said, "You are a dynamic speaker. You have a lot of talent. I don't like your theology, and I don't like the things you were saying. But I like you, and I would like to know you better. Won't you be my guest at lunch today?" We talked 'way into the afternoon. Many more such meetings—some at lunch, some at dinner—followed. I gave my life to Christ, and I deeply appreciate the privilege of standing here and telling what Christ means to me.'"

Dr. Stone continued, "With enthusiasm and zeal he talked to our young people about real dedication and about using every chance they had to make Christ live in someone else's life. He walked down out of the pulpit and challenged all of us to come and stand with him and promise God that from now on we would do all the things that Jesus wanted us to do. With one accord a great crowd of people moved up to stand with him. He lifted his voice and prayed to God to help them carry out the Great Commission, beginning in Baltimore."

God spoke through Isaiah to the Babylonians and to us, but the emphasis is on the right kind of life. He made it very plain that the people of that wicked city were going to be punished and that their city was going to be a Sodom and Gomorrah because they were living like the people who inhabited those two wicked cities. The denunciation God pronounced through Isaiah is far more gentle than it could have been. He didn't say, "Hear this, you who live *wickedly,*" but, "Hear this, you who live *carelessly.*" How like the Master's words when he told the story of the ten virgins—five that were *wise* and five that were *foolish.* We are not of much use to the kingdom of God if we live foolishly or carelessly. Not only may we find the doors of heaven shut against us, but we will find our usefulness to God at a minimum.

I heard a beautiful illustration recently when Dr. Louie D. Newton told me the story of Grace Moore. You may know she was America's sweetheart, not only because she sang so beautifully, but also because she lived beautifully. She bought a palace in Italy, but she didn't invite the disreputable movie crowd to visit her, and she didn't attend their parties. She kept her life clean and close to God. And she was never happier than when she was singing the grand old hymns, such as "Amazing Grace," which she sang to us at the Southern Baptist Convention meeting in Memphis.

Dr. Newton said, "On one occasion she went home to a little mining town in Tennessee to spend Mother's Day with her mother. Since she was front-page news, the reporters and photographers came from all of the nearby cities. They went to the pastor and asked, 'Is she going to sing Sunday, and may we take pictures in the church?' The pastor told them she was not going to sing on Sunday and had very earnestly requested that she not be bothered with interviewers or photographers. She wanted to spend a quiet Sunday in her old home church and sit in the choir seat that she had occupied as a girl. The pastor insisted that no pictures be taken during the church service. They all reluctantly agreed, but they stayed and went to church on Sunday morning.

"The preacher said, 'I knew her mother's favorite song was "In the Garden," so just before time for me to preach, I asked the congregation to remain seated and sing together this grand old hymn. The choir stood as usual, the organist struck the chord, and everybody started to sing. Then everybody stopped except Grace Moore. They had all stopped to listen. She sang each stanza of it. And when she came to the chorus after the last stanza, she had apparently forgotten where she was and everything except the beautiful message of that chorus. And she sang it as if she was singing it to heaven:

> And He walks with me, and He talks with me,
> And He tells me I am His own;
> And the joy we share as we tarry there,
> None other has ever known.

"The pastor said, 'I looked back at those hard-boiled reporters and photographers, and tears were streaming down their faces. In fact, the whole audience had their handkerchiefs out. I knew I couldn't preach after that. We had heard a sermon far better than any I could ever preach. After a long minute in which to get my own voice back, I stood up and announced that the congregation would please stand for the benediction. It was one of those hours that no one would ever forget!' "

I repeat, it was not the voice of Grace Moore, but it was the life back of that voice, that thrilled and stirred an audience. She never lived carelessly, but very, very close to God.

13
Mission Accomplished

Twice recently I have read the words "mission accomplished." Both times they came out of war zones.

One was in connection with the popular wartime song "Coming in on a Wing and a Prayer." They were spoken by the man who led a squadron of planes on a vital and hazardous bombing mission over Germany. Their objective was to destroy a munitions dump. They fought their way through a hailstorm of flak and a swarm of enemy fighter planes. Most of his group of planes were shot down. His own plane was riddled; one wing wobbled, full of holes. He came in low over the water and onto the landing field. The wing crumpled, and the plane skidded as they landed, then turned over. The rescue crew helped him out; and when they noticed the four bloody spots on his uniform, they put him in a jeep and headed for the hospital. He insisted that they take him to the commanding officer first.

He limped into the office, made a ragged salute, and in a husky voice said, "Mission accomplished, sir; but we came in on a wing and a prayer." In a half-audible voice, he repeated, "Mission accomplished," and then he dropped to the floor. They took him on to a hospital, and after weeks of suffering he recovered. His words were repeated in many newspapers; a song writer saw their possibilities and wrote, "Coming in on a Wing and a Prayer." But to many of us the most touching part of that report was "mission accomplished, sir."

I found the words again in a speech made by a chaplain back from the Korean War. A boy had been wounded and hospitalized in Korea. When he was well enough to return home, the chaplain was sent to inform him that there would be a plane out the next day, and another one the day after next, and that he could ride either one of them. The soldier thought a minute and then said, "I'll take the one the day after tomorrow."

"You don't seem to be in a hurry to get home," commented the chaplain.

The soldier replied, "Oh, yes, I am in a hurry, but I have one more thing to do before I go home. There are three Korean boys that our company has been caring for since their mother and father were killed. I want to borrow a jeep from you and take them to a missionary I know. He has a camp, or kind of an orphanage."

The chaplain lent him the jeep and helped him bundle the three boys into it, and they headed south to the missionary's base of operations. When the soldier came back about dusk, the chaplain was waiting for him. "Did you make it all right?" he asked.

With a smile, the soldier answered, "Mission accomplished. I gave that missionary about half of my pay to take care of them." This mission was not a command from his officer, but a command from his heart and from his Heavenly Father. Is there a heart so hard anywhere that is not touched by this soldier's sense of duty and responsibility to the Great Commander?

The words "mission accomplished" can be written over many assignments God gave to his chosen warriors, both in modern days and in Old Testament days.

One of the last speeches that Dr. Robert S. MacArthur, grand old preacher of recent years, made was at Baltimore. It

was the General Ministers' Conference of the big city, and
some six hundred of us packed the church to hear him. He
was helped up to the platform by two pastors. Leaning
against the podium, he said in substance, "As you can all see,
I have about finished my course." Then, with a twinkle in his
eye, he continued: "I hope I have done as good a job as I saw
three boys do in the Southside Baptist Church of Birming-
ham. I was preaching there on a hot Sunday in August. The
downstairs was comfortably filled, but there were only three
boys in the balcony. They sat together on the front seat.

"About halfway through my sermon, there was quite a
commotion in the back of the church. People were twisting
around, and some were smiling. The three boys in the balcony leaned over to see what was making the disturbance. I
followed the line of their gaze and saw a bald-headed man,
who had laid his head on the back of the seat and was fast
asleep, snoring with his mouth wide open. The boys tore a
sheet out of the hymnbook and hastily began making spit-
balls. When they leaned over to take aim, I got over on one
side of the pulpit and began preaching to the people in the
'amen corner.' When I heard a gurgle and a cough, I knew
one of them had hit the target. The boys, well satisfied, sat
back and listened to the sermon." (Mission accomplished.)

Dr. MacArthur spoke on for quite awhile about the assignments that God had given him and about how hard some had
been.

The writer of the book of Joshua bears a wonderful testimony about the leader who succeeded Moses: "Joshua did
. . . as the Lord bade him . . . he left nothing undone of
all that the Lord commanded Moses" (Josh. 11:9–15). That
sentence covers a multitude of trials and tribulations. His
faith was sorely tested when God commanded him to march
around the walls of Jericho until those walls fell down. Over

and over, God commanded him to do what seemed to be impossible tasks. Mission after mission could never have been accomplished by human force and endeavor, but through Joshua's implicit faith in his Heavenly Father, he and God moved mountains and tossed them into the sea.

God told Gideon to take three hundred men, arm them with pitchers, torches, and trumpets, and to conquer that numberless army. Their campfires were as numerous as the sands of the sea. There is one sentence that is unforgettable in the account of the victorious three hundred and their indomitable leader: "They stood every man in his place round about the camp." When the carnage was over and the enemy had fled, in my imagination I can see Gideon looking out across that silent battlefield as he whispered to himself, "Mission accomplished."

There came a day when Paul could see the executioner with his broad-bladed axe waiting to put an end to his life here on earth. There is no whining; instead, there is a note of triumph and joy as he writes to Timothy the immortal words: "I have fought a good fight, . . . I have kept the faith: henceforth there is laid up for me a crown of righteousness, which the Lord, the righteous judge, shall give me at that day: and not to me only, but unto all them also that love his appearing" (2 Tim. 4:7–8).

Now, look at this passage. How beautifully it stands out above all the others in the Old and New Testaments. Jesus, speaking from the cross and "knowing that all things were now accomplished," said, "It is finished." Did he mean his suffering was finished? Did he mean his life on earth was finished? I don't believe he was even thinking about either of these things. He was thinking about his mission. He was thinking about his mission to this earth on which we live. He often referred to the fact that God sent him to do some things here, the most important of which was to carry out his and God's parts in the plan of salvation. His mission of redemption was finished. The last few minutes of his suffering were nearly over. He had paid the penalty for our sins. He had revealed God as a God of love. He had put new meaning into the word "Father" as it referred to the Lord. His mission was accomplished.

There only remained the miracle of the resurrection and the beautiful task of convincing his disciples and hundreds of others that the tomb could not hold him. He had to show them that—despite his crucifixion, death, and burial—he was not dead. The hardships of his mission were over. On every occasion of his appearance after the resurrection, you will find joy, happiness, and rejoicing. He would now return to the Father and send the Comforter in his place.

What a thrilling challenge this is to us, for we, too, have a mission to accomplish. Our missions are different; no two of them are the same, for no two of us are alike. Paul, in that famous letter to the Romans, said:

Having then gifts differing according to the grace that is given to us, whether prophecy, let us prophesy according to the proportion of faith; Or ministry, let us wait on our ministering: or he that teacheth, on teaching; Or he that exhorteth, on exhortation: he that giveth, let him do it with simplicity; he that ruleth, with diligence; he that sheweth mercy, with cheerfulness (Rom. 12:6–8).

I once heard Frank Leavell express this thing in a way that I could never forget. In substance he said, "The world needs to see Jesus, but there is no one of us that can ever paint the picture of Jesus alone. It will take all of us, everyone painting a little part." Then in his humble way he said, "You paint the high lights; I'll paint the shadows." Some of us can show to others the beauty of his countenance; some of us can show the gentleness of his touch; some of us can let them hear the softness of his voice; some of us will have ears to hear the cry of others for help; and some of us can give even as Jesus gave. Since it will take a myriad of people to make the picture complete, God needs everyone. To each of us there is an individual assignment, a mission to accomplish.

Dr. John Maguire, our beloved executive secretary for the Florida Baptist Convention, told of an experience that beautifully illustrates this thought. He was on the faculty of one of the big high schools in Alabama, where he also had charge of athletics and coached the football, baseball, and track teams. He said, "I took the track team down to the state meet one year and saw a most unusual and wonderful thing. The men were lining up for the mile race which, of course, was the big event of the track meet. Since it was rumored that the state record for the mile might be broken that day, an unusually large crowd of spectators had gathered. One of the schools had a most promising miler. Twice at other events he had come within a second of the state record, and he was out to break it this time. As they gathered around the starting mark, all eyes were on that tall, good-looking young man with a gracious smile on his face. He was long of limb and with all the marks of an athlete of the first magnitude.

"Then," Dr. Maguire said, "I saw at the far end of the starting line a boy who was in every way a sharp contrast to this athlete. He was small of stature, his shoulders were bent a little, he was hollow-chested, and even his legs were not straight. I wondered," said Dr. Maguire, "why in the world a school would put a boy like that into the mile race to run against that splendid athlete.

"The command came to 'toe your mark, get set.' Then the pistol cracked and the race was on. The fine athlete sprang into the lead at the very beginning, and with every lap he widened the distance between himself and the others. The little fellow steadily fell behind. When they came into the home stretch, the athlete sprinted the last hundred yards. As he broke the tape, a deafening roar went up from the crowd. He had broken the state record! Only a few others finished the mile; most of the runners had dropped out when they saw it was hopeless for them to win.

"As the field crew were bringing out the hurdles to set up for the next race, suddenly one of the judges yelled, 'Get those hurdles out of the way. This race is not over. Look!' Around the turn came that little boy, panting and staggering. Everybody in the audience stood silently and watched as he dragged up that last hundred yards and literally fell across the finish line. His face ground into the cinder track. One of the judges ran and turned him over on his back, took his handkerchief, and wiped the blood off his face. The judge asked him, 'Son, why didn't you drop out back yonder? What are you doing in the mile race, anyway?'

"Between gasps for breath, the boy answered, 'My school had a good miler, but he got sick two or three days ago and couldn't run. The coach had promised to have a man in every event, so he asked me if I'd come and run the mile.'

" 'Well, son,' the judge continued, 'Why didn't you just drop out, quit 'way back there? You were over half a lap behind.'

"He answered, 'Judge, they didn't send me here to quit. They didn't send me here to win. They sent me here to run this mile, *and I ran the mile.*' " Mission accomplished. Mission accomplished.

14
Earthen Vessels

Dr. Malcolm Lockhart, a grand Episcopal minister, and I were given a trip to Palestine by our respective churches. While in Cairo, we went over to the British Museum. At that time, one of the executives was a retired Episcopal missionary. He was delighted to meet a fellow clergyman from America. He insisted on conducting us personally through the marvelous museum. Dr. Lockhart told him that, since our churches had been gracious enough to give us this trip, we were naturally interested in anything in the big museum that had some spiritual significance. His face lighted up immediately, and he exclaimed, "There are three things that you just must see."

He led us out into the huge foyer of the museum. Around its walls were literally hundreds of marble busts, and some golden goblets which had been used by the Pharaohs. A great crowd of people were milling around, examining the ancient relics. He led us straight to a large alabaster bowl about twelve feet in diameter, which rested on a marble pillar. It was beautiful to look at. Then he said to us, "Walk down to the other end of the hall. You will find another alabaster bowl exactly like this one. Its measurements are precisely the same. Lean over it, but do not touch it. I will whisper in this one, and despite all of the confusion and the din, you can hear distinctly every word I say." We followed his instructions and carried on a whispered conversation with him.

He finished the conversation with a thoughtful question: "Doesn't this illustrate the truth that God can speak to us in that still, small voice even when there is noise and thunder around us; and that we can hear him distinctly, provided our hearts are in perfect tune with his, even as these alabaster bowls are in tune with each other?"

Next, he took us into a room containing many of the things that came from the tomb of one of the Pharaohs. Quietly he said, "Look around you. The people who buried this Pharaoh placed in his tomb everything they thought he might need in the next world. So it is evident they believed in another life, another world, and some form of resurrection. There seems to be born in all mankind the wish, and the conviction, that death is not the end of life."

The next thing he showed us was, to me, the most interesting. It was in the same room. A row of cracked, earthen vessels stood on the most prominent display shelves. He pointed to them and said, "You can see the bottoms of those earthen jars have been sawed off and new clay bottoms have been substituted. These earthen jars were among the golden bowls, pitchers, and goblets in the tomb, and all of the excavators wondered why they had been placed in such a conspicuous position. When the jars were transferred here, they were placed back on the lower shelves, away from the gold and silver and precious stones.

"Then one day an administrator of the museum stopped here for a minute when the afternoon sun, through that western window, shone directly on the clay jars. Something glinted through a crack near the bottom of one jar. His curiosity was aroused. The jar was taken to the office, examined, and finally broken to pieces. You can imagine their surprise when they found that the clay bottom was three inches thick and that imbedded in it were some of the crown jewels of a

Pharaoh. They quickly collected the other earthen vessels and sawed off their bases. When they broke them up, they found the balance of the priceless jewels." The missionary had no explanation for their being hidden like this, but he did have a verse of Scripture. He quoted, "But we have this treasure in earthen vessels, that the excellency of the power may be of God, and not of us" (2 Cor. 4:7).

I thought of this experience and the words of Paul, which the missionary had quoted, many times before I saw the sermon in it. The message divides itself easily into three parts.

The first part concerns the *treasure* about which Paul was talking. He was so full of the message of salvation and the power of the gospel to transform the lives of *everyone* that it bubbles to the top of all of his writings. Over and over, he repeated the message contained in the words of Jesus "him that cometh to me I will in no wise cast out." He realized, more than anyone in his own generation, that the gospel was for *everyone* and that all who received it were "free from the law of sin and death." If Paul had been endowed with power to sing, I think the songs of freedom would have overshadowed all else in his repertoire.

I heard Dale Moody, professor at the Southern Baptist Theological Seminary, speak to a great crowd about the middle wall of partition being broken down. It was a most inspiring message. He drew us a vivid mental picture of what Paul was talking about in his letter to the Ephesians.

Wherefore remember, that ye being in time past Gentiles in the flesh, who are called Uncircumcision by that which is called the Circumcision in the flesh made by hands; That at that time ye were without Christ, being aliens from the commonwealth of Israel, and strangers from the covenants of promise, having no hope, and without God in the world: But now in Christ Jesus ye who sometimes were far off are made nigh by the blood of Christ.

For he is our peace, who hath made both one, and hath broken down the middle wall of partition between us (Eph. 2:11–14).

That middle wall was in the outer court of the temple, and beyond it no Gentile was allowed to pass. On the wall, in Greek, was written; "No Gentile shall pass this wall on penalty of death." So the Publican stood afar off and prayed. The next court was for Jewish women. Then, toward the center was another court, for Jewish men. The next one was for the priests, or Levites. Last of all was the place the high priest alone could enter. It thrilled Paul to be able to stand up and exclaim that "there is neither Jew nor Greek, . . . nor male, nor female" who cannot come all the way to God. Naturally, this great treasure, this gospel, was to him the most glorious thing in the world.

With this picture in mind, we can understand how he thought nothing of the forty stripes save one, the shipwrecks, the jails, and the stocks into which he was placed. No wonder he and Silas could sing at midnight, though their backs were raw. He thought of his body objectively. In his exuberance he once said, "I keep under my body." To him his body was an earthen vessel, and it mattered not if it were chipped and cracked and broken.

The second thought is the reason that Paul likened himself to an earthen vessel. It was, in his words, "to show that the transcending power belongs to God, not to myself" (2 Cor. 4:7, Moffatt).

I found a beautiful illustration of this recently in the biography of Ian Maclaren:

I had been preaching in my first pastorate for a few months when I decided that I should not use notes in the pulpit. So, I wrote my sermon out one week and memorized it. Sunday morning came and I walked into the pulpit a little nervous. I had been preaching only about five minutes when I forgot what came next in my sermon. I stood there embarrassed. The whole congregation fidgeted and were likewise embarrassed. Finally, I said to them, "I tried to memorize my sermon, but I have forgotten it. Will you please sing a song and we will have the benediction?" After the prayer they silently moved out of the church and left me alone. I sat down in the pulpit and wept. Then I got up to go home, but when I came out of the door to my astonishment the congregation were all out in the yard.

Over under a tree the Board of Deacons were standing talking to each other. The Chairman left them and came toward me. I braced myself and said a little prayer. I knew this was it. But when he got close enough for me to see his face, there was a smile on it. The thought flashed through my mind that a man doesn't come to fire you with a smile on his face. He walked up the steps to the door in which I was standing, and put his hands on my shoulders. He spoke in a voice loud enough for everyone to hear, "Don't feel bad because you forgot your sermon. You preach the Word of God like we need it. Keep on memorizing your sermons, if you want to, and the next time you forget just tell us so and let us stand and sing a hymn. You will think of it before we finish the hymn and we will sit down and you can go on preaching." Still smiling, he added, "We all love you and you are God's messenger to us. We know you belong to God."

So, the thing that really matters is the *message*. It is the treasure that is precious and not the stammering delivery or the messenger. The words of Paul in the verses following the text read:

We are troubled on every side, yet not distressed; we are perplexed, but not in despair; Persecuted, but not forsaken; cast down, but not destroyed; Always bearing about in the body the dying of the Lord Jesus, that the life also of Jesus might be made manifest in our body. For we which live are always delivered unto death for Jesus' sake, that the life also of Jesus might be made manifest in our mortal flesh (2 Cor. 4:8–11) .

The earthen vessel is the carrier and the container of the treasure of the gospel.

The message in Paul's mind was that he and all other messengers of God were *expendable*. Nowhere in Paul's writings will you find even a tinge of fear of what might happen to him. He was consumed by one great, driving purpose. He would take the message of salvation and freedom to all the world, if possible. He would go to Spain, to Macedonia, to Rome, or wherever God opened a road. In his letters, oftentimes, you find him imploring those who loved him not to be concerned because he was sick or in bonds or in danger. His one concern was that Jesus Christ should be lived and that he should be preached to all mankind, let it cost what it will in suffering or even death. His own life meant nothing to him. If it had to be broken, that didn't matter.

He expressed it in one of the most beautiful passages of the Bible:

For I am now ready to be offered, and the time of my departure is at hand. I have fought a good fight, I have finished my course, I have kept the faith: Henceforth there is laid up for me a crown of righteousness, which the Lord, the righteous judge, shall give me at that day: and not to me only, but unto all them also that love his appearing (2 Tim. 4:6-8).

Death would be *coronation day* for him. Neither he nor God would have any further use for the old, chipped, cracked vessel in which he and God and the Great Commission had been housed for a few years.

I am afraid most of us do not belong in the same league with Paul. His personal security and comfort meant nothing to him. He was just an earthen vessel—expendable.

There is no modern edition of this consuming zeal that Paul had. The closest of its kind has been recently written about an Australian bushman named Taylor. He has re-claimed about a hundred thousand acres of desert by digging wells and irrigation ditches. Green grass grows where hot sands once smothered all plant life. Someone asked him, "Why do you keep on living out in that hot desert? You are worth twenty-five million dollars. You do not need to work any more. Why don't you take life a little easier?"

His answer reminds me of Paul: "God commissioned me just as he commissioned every missionary and preacher in the world. He commissioned me to turn that desert into a beauti-ful place for people to live. Money? Money doesn't mean any-thing to me. I am not working for money, I am working for God. The money is nothing. As long as God lets me work, I will be turning desert sand into lush green vegetation." It is a rather high step from where most of us live to the place where we can say to our Heavenly Father, "I am just an earthen vessel, and I am expendable."

15
Thirty Pieces of Silver

The first eight verses of Matthew 27 relate one of the most heartbreaking stories in the Bible. It is the story of Judas Iscariot. The tragedy is that it didn't have to happen.

A little pamphlet came to my desk a few months ago. The opening sentence read, "We know, because the Bible tells us, of one man that is surely saved. Jesus said to him on the cross, 'This day shalt thou be with me in paradise.' We know of one man that is surely lost for the Bible tells us so. Jesus in His prayer to His Heavenly Father recorded in John's Gospel, said, 'I've kept all of them that thou hast given me, except the son of perdition, who is lost.'" From the story of Judas Iscariot, four definite messages come right down to earth, right down where we live.

Now, the first one is an answer to questions that I have been asked many times, almost always by young people. Some of them were students at Ridgecrest, others on the campuses of our universities. It worried them. Their fresh, young minds read the story of Judas and asked, "Did Jesus know that Judas Iscariot was going to betray him?" Of course, the answer is yes. The Bible states plainly that he knew from the beginning. "Well, then, what chance did Judas Iscariot have *not* to betray him? Wasn't Judas predestined to betray him? Isn't that plain predestination?" The answer, of course, is no. He wasn't predestined to betray Jesus Christ; there is no predestination here.

I wonder if you have ever turned to your *Cruden's Complete Concordance* and looked up the words "predestinate" and "predestinated"? If you have, you found them only once each in your New Testament, and not at all in the Old Testament. One is found in the eighth chapter of Romans; the other is in the first chapter of Ephesians. And they both say the same thing. Since Paul wrote both letters, your question would be answered forever and forever if you just turned and read those two passages of Scripture. The Romans passage reads:

And we know that all things work together for good to them that love God, to them who are the called according to his purpose. For whom he did foreknow, he also did predestinate to be conformed to the image of his Son, that he might be the firstborn among many brethren. Moreover whom he did predestinate, them he also called: and whom he called, them he also justified: and whom he justified, them he also glorified (Rom. 8:28–30).

God never predestined anyone to do anything that was wicked or wrong. But he does predestine persons to be justified, to be glorified, to be born again, and to be made in the image of his Son. Full many a time, God picks out someone, some man that he needs in the kingdom work like Simon Peter, James, or John. Likewise, God called Daniel, Shadrach, Meshach, Abednego, David, and Samuel. God picked them out for he needed them. Moreover, wherever in the Bible you find the *thought* of predestination, and you will find it in several places, you will find close to it the thought emphasized that man is a free agency.

I have always thought that Judas Iscariot was attracted to Jesus by his beauty, his loveliness, his personality, and the things he taught. There was probably a hunger in Judas's heart for the way of life that Jesus opened before him. Jesus may have used his divine foreknowledge, or he may have used his deep understanding of human nature. For it is written, "And he that searcheth the hearts knoweth what is the mind of the Spirit" (Rom. 8:27). I am sure he knew *someone* would betray him, because his teaching and revelation would upset all of the religious leaders of the day. We should never forget that God knows the future just as we know history. The fact that we know the *past* does not affect what has happened. Nor does the fact that God *knows* the future affect our actions. We are free to choose our way.

Certainly, God often takes the evil that men do and changes it to further his plans. God had no part in the behavior of Joseph's brothers. He could easily have gotten Joseph into Egypt in some beautiful way. But God used the diamond dust of the prison and slavery to polish him and get him ready for the big responsibilities that were eventually dumped on his shoulders.

The second message here is a heartbreaking message but one that we ought to look at closely. *Judas Iscariot sold Jesus out;* you can't read this without feeling a righteous indignation. But, beloved, does it dig deep enough? Is that indignation so deep that *we* won't sell him out? When we remember his own words "Inasmuch as ye have done it unto one of the least of these my brethren, ye have done it unto me," does it dig deep enough to make us rebel immediately against selling Jesus Christ out?

Dr. H. Leo Eddleman told this incident in our church recently. "One Christmas morning about 8:30 my telephone rang. A lady, who wouldn't give me her name, said, 'I have a neighbor who has three children, and there isn't anything in their house to eat this Christmas morning. And there are no toys for the three children. It must be an awful experience for her, and the children are all in tears. She gave me the address and told me the ages of the children. I gathered up a lot of things in my own home, and I called three or four of my deacons, who collected some toys and presents. One of the deacons brought the turkey his family was going to cook for their own dinner. Bless his heart! We made it a real Christmas for them. I asked the mother, just before we left, about her husband.

"She said, 'He's in the penitentiary for attempted murder and robbery.'

"I asked, 'How is it that you don't happen to have any money at all in the house?'

"She answered, 'Our Social Security check didn't come. I reckon they were so busy at Christmas they didn't get it out on time.'

"I continued, 'So your husband is really responsible for the heartache these children are going to remember as long as they live?'

"She sadly nodded her head, 'Yes, yes, my husband was never a Christian. He belonged to the church but was never a Christian.' " He sold Jesus out. He sold him out just as much as Judas Iscariot. Again, "inasmuch as ye have done it unto one of the least of these my brethren, ye have done it unto me."

Dwight L. Moody wrote, "There came to me one day a woman who said, 'Would you please pray for my husband?'

"I told her, 'Certainly. . . . Tell me about him.'

"She said, 'I belong to the church. I'm here every time the door opens, but my husband won't come near the church.'

"I studied her for a moment, then quietly inquired, 'Could I ask you a couple of personal questions?'

"Instantly she replied, 'Of course.'

" 'Do you ever become irritable and say hard things or harsh things to him?'

"Embarrassed, she answered, 'Yes, sir, I'm afraid I'm guilty of that.'

" 'Do you ever become angry and say harsh things to your servants, to your children, or about your neighbors?'

"She hung her head this time, 'Yes, sir, I'm guilty of that too.'

"I said, 'Don't you think I'd better pray for you first?'

"Tearfully, she whispered, 'Yes, sir.' She got down on her knees and I got down on mine and we prayed. About a week later she came back. 'I just have to tell you, Mr. Moody, your questions burned holes in my heart. I got my family together, I got the servants together also, and I told them all that I wasn't the kind of a Christian God wanted me to be, and I was ashamed of it and wanted to ask their forgiveness for every single ugly thing I'd ever said to them. Further, I promised them, with God's help, I would never say them any more. I asked them to forgive me. We all got to crying, and we all got down to pray.

"My husband prayed aloud, 'Dear Jesus, I give my life to you this day. I want to be the kind of a Christian my wife wants to be.' "

Beloved, have we sold him out in our homes? Have we let him down and become just as inconsistent as those Pharisees when Judas Iscariot brought back those thirty pieces of silver and threw them down at their feet? He told the Pharisees he didn't want the money, that he had betrayed an innocent man. Heartlessly, they sneered, "What is that to us?"

Then they gathered up the scattered pieces of silver, and one of them remarked, "We can't put these back in the treasury. It's blood money." But they could use it to kill Jesus with—rank inconsistency! Beloved, what Jesus needs greatly today is consistency in Christian thinking, in Christian attitudes, and in Christian living.

It just might be that some of us need to say, "My attitude toward the church, and toward some of the people there, is not right. I want all of you in my home to forgive me, and I want God to forgive me." It just might be that we are letting him down as Judas let him down.

Now, take the third observation. I don't think Judas Iscariot got suddenly to the place where he sold Jesus out. I think there was a progressiveness in his sin. I think it was a long, gradual process. Someone wrote a drama years ago with the title "The World's Slow Stain." It brought to mind the story of Saul and David and Goliath. When David killed the giant, Saul's heart went out to the handsome young hero. He would take David home and adopt him. Henceforth, he would eat at the King's table. All went well until the women, who had lined both sides of the road to welcome the victorious army home, began to sing, "Saul hath slain his thousands, and David his ten thousands." The little green imp of jealousy was planted in the mind of Saul. It grew and grew and grew. At first, it was a tiny plant, but it finally grew so big that it absorbed his whole life. Then, as with Judas, it brought him to an ignoble death.

A country preacher said, "I stopped to see one of my members, a fine old farmer, who was getting ready to plow a field. I pulled my buggy up, got out, and walked over to where he was standing. I asked, 'What are you fixing to do?'

"He said, 'I'm fixing to plow up the grass and turn it under down here between these corn rows.'

"I looked and said, 'I can't see any grass.'

"He sorta' smiled. 'Preacher,' he said, 'you know perfectly well the grass is there. You get down close enough, and you can see a little of it, but a lot of it has already sprouted. I'm going to turn it over before it gets to be grass and absorbs the fertilizer and the strength of the soil. I'm going to turn it over so it will never grow. I want that corn to have all of the strength in the soil.' "

Do you want Jesus Christ to have all of you? Then there might be some weeds that need to be pulled up and thrown out of your very heart and soul, for they will grow and ruin your life. I think this evil spirit grew in Judas Iscariot. Certainly, when he started following Jesus, it wasn't noticeable. The first evidence that we have of it was when he objected to some ointment being sprinkled on Christ and said it was wasted. He said it ought to have been sold, but the disciple who wrote the event down said it was because Judas kept the bag and he wanted the money for himself because he was a thief.

Someone told of a man who realized, when he was about fifty-five, that he was pretty irritable in the home and that he often said some mean things to his wife and to others. One day he repented and made her this promise: "From this minute on, I will never say another unkind thing to you as long as I live." His own confession was that "I never broke that promise more than a thousand times." He added, "You know, after something grows in you for fifty-five years, you can't get rid of it suddenly. It becomes a part of your personality." So we ought to watch our hearts to see what's growing there, and we ought not let anything grow that isn't beautiful and good and fine. The evil in Judas grew slowly but surely.

Now, the last message. And I wish I could say this last one like it's in my heart to say it. Judas Iscariot hanged himself, but Judas Iscariot *didn't need to hang himself*. The story didn't need to end that way. The facts didn't need to be that way. Simon Peter sold out, too, but he didn't hang himself. Now, would you turn your imagination loose a minute and let me tell the story as it might have been? I think it might have been this way. On the shores of the Sea of Galilee, where Jesus told his disciples to meet him, Simon Peter said, "I'm going fishing."

The others said, "We are going with you." And while they were out there fishing, there came down to the Sea of Galilee the quiet, poised figure of Jesus Christ. Standing in the semi-darkness, he watched his beloved disciples as they cast their nets and hauled them in empty. He didn't see the man who was about fifty or seventy-five yards away, sitting in the sand with his elbows on his knees and his face in his hands. He'd been watching them, too, but he knew better than to ask them to let him go with them. They wouldn't have anything to do with him. He had sold Jesus out. He was Judas Iscariot.

He hadn't seen Jesus. And the first time he knew Jesus was there was when he heard the voice he had learned to love ask the fishermen, "Have you any meat? Have you caught anything?"

They answered, "No, we've toiled all night and caught nothing."

"Well, put your net down on the other side of the boat." Slowly, Judas got to his feet and walked toward the Master. Then he dropped to his knees, put his arms around the feet of Jesus, and sobbed. He spoke not a word; he really didn't need to say anything. He just knelt and wept. He felt the hand of Jesus on his head, and in a moment the quiet voice of Jesus said, "Judas, thy sins be forgiven thee. Get up. I'm going to call the others in. I've got a big job for all of you to do. I want you twelve men to take the story of the kingdom of God to the world."

Beloved, that's the way it might have been; that's the way it should have been. It didn't have to end as it did. That's the way it might have been. That's the way it might be for every one of us. The Bible tells us that Judas repented, but that wasn't enough. He took the money back and flung it down on the floor. He wouldn't have it. He was filled with remorse, shame, and sorrow, and he repented for the thing he had done. But that wasn't quite enough. He needed, and we need, to come back and fall at the feet of Jesus. Probably, we won't need to say a word; he'll understand. But we need to come back to him. Repentance never saved anyone. It's part of the great plan of salvation, but it's not all of it, not nearly all of it. We need to take one more step. That one step could be the difference between eternal doom and eternal life. Jesus came to seek and to save that which was lost; and he is "the same yesterday, and to day, and for ever."